Undercover Drug Agent: A Walk of Faith

Joe,

Thank you for your service. Always remember, If God be for us, who could be against us!

[signature]

Undercover Drug Agent: A Walk of Faith

R. DARRELL WEAVER

ISBN: 1537221582
ISBN 13: 9781537221588
Library of Congress Control Number: 2016914741
CreateSpace Independent Publishing Platform
North Charleston, South Carolina

Table of Contents

Introduction

This book is about the seedy world of drug trafficking and the valiant agents who get up everyday and work to combat the scourge, but most importantly it showcases good vs. evil. A loving God who wants good for the world is pitted daily against the devil who wants to destroy the world. The names in this book were changed, but all is factual. I could have written hundreds more chapters based on the many drug deals and enforcement operations I participated in, but these chapters will give you a compelling look at the way it is. I am an imperfect man who serves and trusts in an awesome, perfect God. I don't deserve God's goodness, but I receive it anyway.

I want to thank my wife Kim for her constant support and love. You are the love of my life, and I adore you. To my children, thank you for believing in your Dad, the dreamer. To my editor, LaVonna Funkhouser, you were a godsend, and we are a perfect match. Your attention to detail is amazing. Thank you Michael Harris for the cover and giving my idea a needed boost. Most importantly, I thank my Lord and Savior Jesus Christ. You are truly my strength, my fortress, and my high tower. I give You the glory!

1

THE CALLING

I could feel the sweat running down my face and clouding my ability to see through the binoculars. If only I could get a good look at the trailer house perched fifty yards away in the heavy tree line and gather a fraction more evidence. We were so close to having sufficient probable cause to secure an affidavit and search warrant for the suspected methamphetamine laboratory. I was nervous, my prone position behind the tree was uncomfortable, and it did not help that every time I moved, I managed to make contact with a piece of hard steel on my CAR-16 rifle. However, I did find solace knowing my faithful machine gun was beside me in the event of a gun fight.

Only a few hours earlier, the subject surprised us as the surveillance creep team covertly made our way through the thick bushes. The trees and dense shrubs had concealed the sound of his beater truck as he turned the corner on the dirt trail. In a split second without us realizing it, he was on us, and we dove behind anything to keep from being seen and prevent our surveillance from being compromised. Our camouflaged clothing and quick reaction must have worked. Miraculously, he did not see us.

He stopped the truck and rolled a canister out the back into what appeared to be a trash dump site. He did not linger long and was soon back in the truck, heading down the small dusty path. He was gone as swiftly as he arrived. My heart finally stopped racing; a near miss and everyone was safe.

He left us wondering. What did he drop off in the dump? Could it help our case? Methodically, the small team of three made our way to the pile of debris. I spotted the cardboard canister and read the inscription on it, "Phenylacetic Acid." We hit the jackpot! This unique chemical is the main precursor in the manufacturing of methamphetamine. It is the chemical that produces the horrible odor associated with the illicit labs. This distinct smell is hard to describe, but once the stench reaches your nostrils, your brain will not soon forget it.

I swatted another mosquito as I focused the binoculars one more time. I heard Senior Agent Leroy Glass radio me on my handheld walkie-talkie. He was located at the District Attorney's office in a neighboring county preparing the document as I relayed to him our evidence. Boosted by a repeater, the walkie-talkie allowed us to communicate clearly despite the approximately 20 miles that separated us.

As my vision and focus became remarkably clear, I saw another canister on the porch of the mobile home. I could read the markings, "Phenylacetic Acid," and now this important chemical was tied directly to the residence. Bingo, we finally had enough to proceed with a warrant. I relayed the information to Agent Glass. But wait, as I scanned I noticed an object protruding out of the top of the trailer house. It couldn't be! I thought, "Am I delusional?" I put everything I had into focusing on the object and brought the scope of the binoculars even tighter and was positive now on what I saw. It was true. A condenser tube was sticking out of the roof of the trailer house, another key part of a lab. Cooks would attach the tube to the round-bottom flask during the manufacturing process. We thought we hit the jackpot before, but now we hit the mega win. You can't have any better evidence than a condenser tube poking through the top of a trailer house roof.

I immediately radioed Agent Glass and told him my discovery. Agent Glass then basically told me I had lost my mind. He knew I had been on the surveillance for several days and believed now I was simply delusional. Finally, after several minutes of intense discussion, I point blank told him to add it in the affidavit as I was positive what I saw on top of the residence. Reluctantly, he finally gave in and included the information fact in the affidavit.

After two long days of gathering evidence, the warrant was signed. We teamed up and hit the place to secure the residence. What we found in the back bedroom was almost unbelievable, the largest round-bottom flask cooking meth that we had ever seen. The whole bedroom was nothing but a huge triple neck boiling flask, which created a great mystery of how they even got it in the room. Walls must have come down to get that humungous vessel in that tight spot. And yes, the condenser tube was sticking through the top of the roof just as I had reported. Unfortunately, the suspect was not there, but days later he would be caught and brought to justice.

Now we had to process and dismantle the lab, but the adrenaline was gone. The nights without sleep were now relevant, as we were tired and hungry. The local chemist arrived to help and brought us pizza. By the way, still today, that was the best pizza I have ever eaten in my life. The nutrition gave us the second wind we needed as we started processing the lab. Under the direction of the chemist, we assisted in the cleanup of the lab. You have to remember that narcotics agents can be dangerous with chemicals.

Truthfully, agents can be dangerous with just about anything. During the cleanup, someone accidently mixed an acid and a base. This was not good, and the container in the back of the pickup started taking on a life of its own. The jug started to boil and expand as we all ran for cover. It exploded just as agents were bailing out of the back of the pickup. The toxic foam even splattered in an agent's face! His sight was probably saved by his eye glasses.

This meth lab and surveillance experience was just a snapshot of what I would experience the next twenty-eight years. I would endure a hundred-thousand more hours of watching and waiting. Such excitement was the life of an undercover drug agent—a life most can only imagine.

Many of us come to a point in our lives when we realize we are not going to be a professional athlete. We just simply do not have the talent to secure our name on the roster of a professional team. As a football quarterback, I dreamed of being the next Roger Staubach or Fran Tarkenton, winning the Super Bowl, and hoisting up the Vince Lombardi Trophy. Sometimes we have the heart, but not the skill. I fell into that category. I found myself searching for direction in my life and asking hard questions like, "What am I going to do with my life?" A family friend once told me that the people who learn the numbers often run the organization. To a young man, that was very intriguing. Don't we all want to run the organization? Of course we do. So I moved back to southwest Oklahoma and started the accounting program at Cameron University in Lawton.

I have to admit, in high school I was an average student and did not apply myself at a high level. I may have been the only high school student who never took a book home to study in the history of Comanche High, but for some reason I was always very good in mathematics, and numbers have always come easily to me. My plan was to learn accounting, make stacks of money, and sail off into the sunset! Little did I know that accounting was one of the tougher undergraduate degrees of study. Many students start in accounting, but after a short tenure, change majors and embrace less rigorous subjects.

Accounting I and Accounting II are relatively easy, and most students pass these courses with little difficulty. However, Intermediate Accounting I is a different beast. It is ferocious. Students said that academia missed a mandatory class and possibly a book or two between Accounting II and Intermediate I. We were left feeling lost when we got to this gap in instruction. I always believed it was actually by design and was intended to cull students from the accounting program. I was determined to pass Intermediate, and eventually, after a grueling semester, I survived with a passing grade.

After Intermediate Accounting, the courses eventually became easier, and I settled into the program. For some reason, I always seemed somewhat out of place in the field of accounting. An old saying about "a bull in a china closet" describes how I felt. Intellectually, great cohorts populated the program, and I respected the type of dedicated student who was attracted to the accounting profession. Even though I was very much out of place in this field, I did recognize the value of learning the numbers in an organization, and I knew that it would benefit me. Something deep in my heart told me I needed more adventure in my life.

Life is short and man's days are numbered. James Chapter 4:14 (NIV) says, "What is your life? You are a mist that appears for a little while and then vanishes." Yes indeed, we are a vapor, and I had to find real contentment and direction in my life. I had to find and embrace what God's plan was for my life. Little did I know that very soon my path would reveal itself to me and I would never be the same.

December 14, 1984, was the end of the semester, and I was looking forward to the Christmas break. As dawn broke that day, my life would forever change. Geronimo is a small community near Lawton in southwest Oklahoma—a community of approximately 800 people who appreciate small-town life and who want to get away from the hustle and bustle of the city. Like many small communities in Oklahoma, Geronimo is a sleepy town that embraces family, faith, and hard work in a safe environment, where front doors were not locked until bedtime and kids safely wandered small-town streets with confidence and security. How suddenly life can change! On this fateful day, two individuals walked into the local bank and created chaos. Jay Wesley Neill and Robbie Grady Johnson had the specific intent to rob the bank, but the result was much more destruction than a simple robbery. Four people were horribly murdered that day, and several others were injured. It shocked not only a community, but a state, and a nation. This crime will forever be known as the "Geronimo Bank Killings."

We must realize this crime was committed prior to the world-changing events of September 11, 2001, when America was under terrorist attack, and even before the horrific bombing of the Oklahoma City Alfred P. Murrah Federal Building on April 19, 1995, where 168 people lost their lives. The period before the Geronimo bank killings was a time of innocence, but evil now had exposed itself. Small-town Oklahoma was threatened and in a panic.

Neill and Johnson fled the scene and the Federal Bureau of Investigation led a massive manhunt. People in Oklahoma were in fear. This simply does not happen in our state. People were shocked and dismayed. Eventually, the investigation took authorities to San Francisco, California, where Neill and Johnson were captured. Jay Wesley Neill was convicted of the crime and sentenced to death. On December 12, 2002, almost 18 years to the date of the Geronimo bank killings, Neill was put to death by lethal injection in McAlester, Oklahoma. Robbie Grady Johnson was also convicted but sentenced to life without the possibility of parole within the Oklahoma Department of Corrections. Although justice was served, lives were lost, and the innocence of small-town Oklahoma was buried forever.

I was captivated by the investigation. I followed it eagerly, watching, reading, and listening for every detail of law enforcement's pursuit of the perpetrators. I quickly realized how important law-enforcement was to society and how they were on the front lines of good versus bad. Law enforcement was standing in the gap for a civil world and justice; what an incredible responsibility! At that moment in my life, I realized I found my calling. I did not know how, when, or where, but I knew I must be in law enforcement. This was where I belonged. It was my God-given, God-driven calling. What a release to know I had made one of the most significant discoveries in my life!

However, I had no family in this profession. My great-grandfather was not a former county sheriff, nor was my uncle a past police officer. In many professions, family members follow in each other's footsteps. This was not the case for me. I had no one to counsel me and had no real direction, but despite this, I knew the desires of my heart and felt very strongly God had put that calling deeply into my spirit.

I had so much time and hard work invested in my accounting degree that I decided to persevere and finish the course of study and graduate. However, I started to explore avenues to allow me to start my gun-toting career. Law enforcement is like any profession, if you have experience, you have an advantage. How do you get the advantage without having the opportunity for experience? I started to explore different options at municipal, state, and federal levels. Knowing that I was obtaining an accounting degree, I started looking at the Federal Bureau of Investigation. The FBI investigated white-collar crimes and hired many accountants and lawyers. I soon realized that they normally accepted applicants with prior law enforcement experience, thus I knew I had to look elsewhere. I wanted to stay in Oklahoma as this state had always been endeared to my heart, and because the events that originally peaked my interest in the field were here. I also knew that it would be hard to leave my family and strong friendships I had developed over the years, so I eliminated federal agencies as possible prospects.

During my research, I discovered the investigative agencies in the State of Oklahoma were all separate entities. One particular agency caught my attention that seemed like it would be challenging and thrilling! The agency was a relatively small drug enforcement agency named the Oklahoma Bureau of Narcotics and Dangerous Drugs Control. Most people simply called the agency the Oklahoma Bureau of Narcotics or OBN for short. The 1980's was a time in our nation's history when First Lady Nancy Reagan was very engaged in policy issues about illicit drugs. Mrs. Reagan had an anti-drug slogan, "Just Say No," which encouraged demand reduction among our children and young people. The term "demand reduction" means simply keeping young people off drugs by educating them of the consequences. The nation was recognizing the destruction of substance abuse and its terrible impact on society. Like many programs, the awareness brought funding, and funding led to hiring agents, which meant employment. Thus, the Oklahoma Bureau of Narcotics, as an agency, was in an expansion phase and hiring new drug enforcement agents. I made an inquiry and discovered that during the last semester of a college degree, one could take the merit test for the entry-level drug agent position. The test scores would be ranked, and for every open position, the agency would interview 10 applicants on the roster. In another words, scoring well was critical to rank as high on the roster as possible.

I started testing for the Agent I position, which did not require any previous law enforcement experience. Along with me, hundreds of other applicants were competing for only a few positions. The competition was intense. Test questions were over basic law enforcement, investigative techniques, the English language, mathematics, and a variety of other topics including handling of evidence, criminal procedure, interrogations, and overall criminal justice.

As an accounting major, I admittedly had limited education in many of the testing areas, but I had to make it up with effort, perseverance, and heart. I devised a crude strategy in an attempt to improve my testing score with each attempt. I drove approximately 82 miles from southwest Oklahoma to Oklahoma City to take the standard test. The rule stated that one could take the test every 30 days in an attempt to improve their score, so I was committed not to miss an opportunity to test. Most importantly, I was going to improve my score each time I tested. Improvement was key if I expected to achieve the next step, an oral interview. I pondered the dilemma of "how." Finally, I developed a system. When I tested, I would memorize the questions to which I was unsure of the correct response. After the test, I would sprint to my car and document as many of the questions that I could remember. Then I would research each one, preparing for the next test. I had a designated notebook for my system. Thank goodness the system worked, and I began to increase my score until after four times I achieved my goal and made it nearly to the top of the roster!

In the meantime, I was blessed with an incredible opportunity with Halliburton Services as an accountant. Halliburton is a worldwide oil services company that has strong Oklahoma roots, and the company founder, Earl P. Halliburton, headquartered the company in Duncan, Oklahoma for many years. They had not hired an accountant in several years, yet I got the call to go to work for them in their report section. The job was a blessing from God. I will always be grateful for that first opportunity. I witnessed corporate America at work, up close and personal, and it was interesting. I actually found the work at Halliburton in the report section very challenging, but I knew it was not my calling. I knew I would not be fully content until I followed my passion as a law enforcement officer.

Finally, I received the letter I had been waiting for since college graduation! It was a date to go to Oklahoma City before the oral interview board at the Oklahoma Bureau of Narcotics and Dangerous Drugs Control. I was a nervous wreck. I had full confidence that God was with me, but sometimes a person is just plain nervous. I anxiously drove to Oklahoma City, and arrived at OBN headquarters, a peculiar environment. As I looked around the room, I saw long-haired, bearded men who looked like they were throwback hippies. I was fascinated knowing that these folks walked among us as citizens, but we had no idea they were some of the most elite law enforcement in the profession. I was surrounded by strangers, who ironically, decades later would become my partners as close as family, and the Bureau would become my second home.

I walked through the doors of the Lincoln Plaza building and was escorted to a large conference room where five agents and the Director, Tom Heggy, were waiting. I did not know anyone in the room, but I did recognize Director Heggy. He was the retired police chief of the Oklahoma City Police Department, and I had read several articles he had written in police journals. He had authored several books and held numerous advanced degrees. He was somewhat of a celebrity in the law enforcement world.

The Lord always gives us peace in times of trouble. As I look back at that interview, I remember there was a peace about me as I answered their questions. John 14:27 (NIV) says, *"Peace I leave with you; my peace I give you. I do not give to you as the world gives. Do not let your hearts be troubled and do not be afraid."* I had a peace only the Lord can give. I was determined. I took a deep breath and pushed forward. At the conclusion of the interview, I respectfully said to the board, "I'm not going to give up. If you don't hire me this time, you will see me again."

I was later told by one of the board members that my final statement was what placed me over the top in the selection process. After I left that day, the waiting began, and it seemed like an eternity before I heard from the agency. Finally, the human resources specialist contacted me to advise they were beginning the background investigation, and an agent would be contacting me. At that point, I started pondering everything I had ever done wrong, and I wanted to believe that my minor mischief would not be a disqualifier. After all, I drove a lot of fast cars in high school and had several minor traffic violations. I was hopeful that my minor stint as a youthful Stephens County NASCAR driver would not inflict a crash on my career before the first green flag. I completed the background questionnaires with the plan that I would pray hard and throw myself on the mercy of the court.

It seemed like an eternity, but a month later I received a call that the background investigator wanted to do an in-house visit with me. Senior Agent Jake Davis arrived and conducted the interview. Many years later, Jake and I would become good friends. We had a mutual love for the martial arts, education, and music. Jake was extremely intelligent, and eventually in his career obtained a PhD. However, at this time, all I knew was this individual, Senior Agent Davis, was asking many questions, writing copious notes, and would report back the status of Darrell Weaver as a prospective OBN Agent.

Jake was always a friendly type, and I remember he made me feel at ease. After I survived his battery of questions, he gathered his notebook and headed to his car. I was worried about the traffic tickets, so before he drove out of the driveway I walked back to his vehicle. I pointedly asked him if the tickets were going to be an automatic disqualification to becoming an agent. Again, with Jake's good nature, he smiled and said, "Probably not, we've all had a few outlaw days in our past." I went back into the house and had great confidence that I would get hired as an agent with the Bureau, yet I knew I had several hurdles still to go.

My next contact with the agency was to schedule my polygraph examination. Polygraphs are a strange phenomenon. I truthfully do not know of anyone who would not be nervous as he or she is strapped with massive wiring attached to this machinery. One is anxious even if he or she is totally innocent. I had nothing to hide, but I still dreaded the process. However, I was confident I would pass. I journeyed late one evening back to Oklahoma City, and the agency polygrapher conducted his business on me, or should I say a wet, sweaty me. I do not sweat a lot, but I must admit taking a polygraph made me sweat. Through all the nerves, I completed the task at hand and was told years later that my polygraph chart was one of the cleanest and most precise results that the long-time, seasoned polygrapher had ever seen. I passed with flying colors, another high hurdle down!

Finally, after a laborious process and weeks of waiting, I received the letter that I had been waiting for with great anticipation. The letter offered me a position with the OBN, and I could hardly contain my excitement! I did not know what tomorrow held, but I knew who held my tomorrows. My confidence was firmly in my Lord and I knew He was ordering my steps as promised in Psalms 37:23 (KJVA), *The steps of a good man are ordered by the Lord: and he delighteth in his way.*" God had helped me and I was thankful. Don't fret in life. God helped me, and He will help you. He holds us in the palm of His hand.

I selected a September 14 reporting date to start my new career as that would allow me a two-week notice to Halliburton. Because they had shown me favor, my apprehension level was high as I thought about resigning my position at Halliburton. Nervously, I walked into the manager's oversized office. It felt like it was a 2,000 square foot space. His desk appeared as large as a billiard table without the corner pockets. He was a gray-haired, stately gentleman who always seemed to be approachable, but truthfully I had little contact with him. Our only previous meeting was at my hiring interview, and now I was sitting across from him about to tell him that I was leaving. I began pouring my heart out to him about the calling I felt and the desire to pursue my passion in life. I will never forget his response, his kindness, and specific words. He told me that I reminded him of his son, then he smiled a big smile and told me, "Chase your dreams. If it doesn't work out, you can always come back. I will put you back to work."

Later in years, I adopted the same supportive philosophy this manager used on me, and I supported young men and women to chase their dreams. Halliburton was a great job. Frankly, I took a reduction in salary by taking an agent position, but I was not motivated by money. There are more important things in life than to chase the almighty dollar. My step of faith was that I fulfill my God-given calling and let the Lord worry about the finances. Psalms Chapter 50 declares that God owns the cattle on a thousand hills. That's some pretty fat stacks! We have a tendency to place emphasis on money and material things, but God couldn't care less.

On September 14, 1987, I reported to the Oklahoma Bureau Narcotics Lawton District office. I had no way of foreseeing the many years of adventure that were ahead. It didn't take long to realize the robust nature of narcotics enforcement. My very first day, my Senior Agent, Leroy Glass, needed to travel to Mangum, Oklahoma, to interview a confidential source incarcerated in the Greer County Jail.

Oklahoma is the 20th largest state geographically in the United States and covers 69,960 square miles. It is a large state with a lot of ground to cover as a state agency. Mangum was approximately 80 miles from Lawton, and Agent Glass requested OH–6 spotter/reconnaissance aircraft support from the Oklahoma National Guard counter drug unit to fly us to Mangum. I had never ridden in a helicopter before in my life, and I was extremely excited! We lifted off, and I was like a kid in a candy store. I couldn't believe it! Here I was, a young man from Comanche, Oklahoma, flying in a helicopter as an OBN Agent. Oklahoma gets very hot, and this particular day was a scorcher in excess of 100 degrees! This is the kind of heat that can cook an egg on a sidewalk. In addition, the OH-6 aircraft had a hydraulic leak providing a heavy petroleum odor in the bird. Add the fact that when growing up I could not even ride in the backseat of my family's car without getting carsick, and the ingredients were adding up to a not-so-pretty result. Here I am, 6 feet 1 inch tall, cramped in the back of a stinky, tremendously hot, spinning-like-a-top helicopter with no tricks up my sleeve to stop the swirling in my stomach. I held on and fended off the sickness as we landed, and I felt better as I got to stand on my own two feet. I was on the ground, but admittedly my head was still spinning.

We went to the jail and interviewed the confidential source. My first glimpse into the drug world was fascinating. I was sitting in the interview room when they brought him in and sat him across from me. He looked to be around fifty-five years of age but later I would learn that he was only in his early forties. It was my first look at how drugs aged an individual and made them look much older than they actually were. A distinct example of a hard life of substance abuse was now sitting before me. We were required to complete a history sheet on any interview we conducted and drill down on prior drug use. The source stated without hesitation that he had used, abused, and distributed every drug known to man. I specifically asked him if he had ever used heroin. His answer shocked me. He said, "Yes I have used heroin, as much as a bathtub full!" Wow, a bathtub full of heroin, that's a lot of heroin! I knew very little at this point about the drug world, but I knew that amount had to be a lot.

We completed the interview and were hungry, so we decided to stop at the SONIC Drive-in for a quick bite to eat. By this time, I had survived the initial helicopter ride and my first drug informant interview. I was feeling pretty confident as an Agent. I made a command decision my stomach was fine, and proceeded to eat a nice, thick cheeseburger. By the way, SONIC makes an excellent cheeseburger! If you have never had one, you must partake.

After lunch, we reboarded the helicopter and started our return flight to Lawton. I soon realized I made my first tactical error. I should not have eaten the cheeseburger! It was just too much for a "seasoned" narcotics agent of fewer than 6 hours to overcome, and I started getting airsick. Embarrassed, I spoke up and told the pilot over the headset I was getting sick and asked if he could set the aircraft down on the ground. We were only flying at approximately 1,000 feet, but it felt like 30,000 feet. For my swirling stomach, the ground did not come fast enough. I think I would have been fine if we would have been at 800 feet and maybe even 900 feet. Apparently, I wasn't fine at 1,000 feet as right before we landed, I got sick. It was not pretty! Thank goodness for the SONIC cup! The pilot and Senior Agent Glass handled it well and didn't give me a hard time over the minor setback. My first day as a superhero crime fighter and I get sick on the chopper! That yummy cheeseburger didn't taste nearly as good the second time coming up as it did the first time going down. Life has a way of humbling a person.

Little did I know that was only the start of the wild ride I would experience in the next many years in pursuit of fulfilling my destiny. My calling became a law enforcement commission, then a commitment as a public servant and the quest to make a difference in this world. I was reminded of the words Jesus said, *"Anyone who puts a hand to the plow and then looks back is not fit for the kingdom of God."* My hand was securely on the plow, and I was never turning back in my life.

2

THE FIRST DRUG DEAL

The general public has an illusion that undercover narcotics agents and vice officers somehow have a personal lifestyle in the drug world prior to becoming an agent. They think because the agents have to adapt undercover and take on identities as drug dealers that prior drug world involvement would be an advantage. This could not be further from the truth. The reality is that because of the nature and temptations of the job, the drug enforcement agent has to exhibit impeccable character and have no prior drug use. Thus they undergo a vigorous preemployment background investigation and mandatory polygraph. "Be sure your sins will find you out" applies here. Integrity is the most important character trait of a narcotics agent. You can train anyone but you cannot "train" integrity. We handle large sums of cash, guns, informants, and drugs, and when one deals with these items, one must have a moral compass to navigate his or her actions and responses.

I was the middle child of five children raised in Comanche, Oklahoma, a small community in southwest Oklahoma with a population of approximately 2,000 people. My mother fought her demons, but she raised us with honor, integrity, and a much needed moral compass. Corralling five children on Sunday morning to attend Sunday school and worship service was a challenge for mom, but she managed to pull it off. We were always in church every time the doors opened. I remember one of my siblings asked our mother, "Mom, are we going to church today?" She answered with a question, "Are you going to school Monday?" We always knew the answer. Proverbs 22:6 (KJVA) says, *"Train up a child in the way he should go: and when he is old, he will not depart from it."* My mother was very dogmatic. I am so glad she forced us to attend church and introduced us to Jesus Christ. It was the greatest gift a parent could ever give us, and I am and always will be grateful.

Because of my upbringing, my mother would have literally been furious if we kids entangled ourselves in drugs. The outcome would not have been pleasant. I lived a very sheltered life with little exposure to anything criminal. I was naïve when it came to anything having to do with the dark and seedy drug world. Since drug agents are required to have such a clean background, we have an enormous learning curve when it comes to illicit drug operation functionality. We must learn rapidly and pick up things quickly.

In the first year as an undercover narcotics agent, we spend the majority of our time training in a formal setting and on-the-job training. Nothing prepares us faster than on-the-job training and observing how to do the basic function of enforcement work. We watch, listen, and absorb critical information like a sponge. The drug world is different than most occupations, and it is not forgiving when mistakes are made. One false read while undercover could lead to injury or death. One lapse while conducting surveillance for a fellow agent could jeopardize that agent's safety and could lead to unpleasant things happening to them.

One critical way of learning is to listen to the senior agents' stories they tell as they climbed the ranks. In law enforcement, we call these types of stories "war stories," and I must admit that sometimes the stories grow exponentially as the years go by, similar to fishing stories. Today, it's a nine-pound bass that fought like a bull shark, but reality is the small perch didn't really put up much of a battle. Time has a tendency to make stories more dynamic. Also, it is amazing how many agents were present during big events or drug deals. The crowd grows, and there must have been a hundred agents on that shootout. However, I gained tremendous value and learning experience by listening to the older agents' mistakes and how they handled certain situations.

Being an agent is almost like a high-stakes game where you try to outsmart the bad guy in the drug transaction. A critical component is staying alive in the process. We say of the junior narcotics agent that for the first couple of years, the primary focus is to keep the agent alive. In any job, mistakes are made early in your career, but you discover quickly that the opportunity for mistakes is very narrow and has to be almost completely eliminated to survive. Agents have simply no wiggle room for a strategic mishap. An uncalculated risk is never welcomed.

Drug dealers, traffickers, and co-conspirators are a group of people who live in the shadowy parts of society. Their world is dark and dirty. Drug dealers desire power and control, but the primary motivator is the almighty dollar. 1 Timothy 6:10 (NIV) says, *"For the love of money is a root of all kinds of evil. Some people, eager for money, have wandered from the faith and pierced themselves with many griefs."* This is never truer than with drug dealers. They love money and will do anything to profit off the backs of addicts and accelerate evil. Greed is a powerful tool and is very dangerous when it infiltrates a soul.

A tremendous amount of money can be made in the drug world, and the profit margins are extremely lucrative. In other words, for a very nominal investment, a drug dealer can turn a massive profit on a relatively small amount of drugs. Dealers that deal in large amounts are normally called "quantity" dealers, and they make their profits by selling a highly pure product in large quantities, normally in pounds or kilos. This type of dealer is more insulated because they have fewer people they are dealing directly within the supply chain. In general, higher quantity dealers are closer to the source of the drug. Smaller quantity dealers normally buy the product in the largest quantity they can afford. Sometimes it is pound quantities and at other times it could be quarter pound quantities. At the lowest level, a street dealer could sell even smaller quantities such as quarter papers of methamphetamine or cocaine, which would represent a quarter gram of product. Paper is the slang for money, which means that you would get a quarter gram of product for around twenty-five bucks.

The midrange dealers often deal in ounces of powdered products like methamphetamine and cocaine. They will take the product and purchase a "cutting agent," which will be added to the product to increase the weight, thus increasing the amount of product they have available for resale. For example, they could take an ounce of methamphetamine and add an ounce of "cut" and now have two ounces of meth to peddle, which would double their profit. Also, the smaller quantities the dealers distribute increase profits as they can cut it more and have even more to sell. The problem is that the more the drug is diluted by a cutting agent, the less effective it is to the end-user. Therefore, a dealer has to be careful not to weaken the product to the point where people would not purchase it. In addition, the drug dealers assume a higher level of risk to be caught by law enforcement if they have a distribution network that deals with a high volume of people. One of the primary objectives of a drug-dealing organization is to avoid law enforcement and incarceration, which could stop, or at minimum slow down, their organization. Unfortunately, most established drug distribution networks can continue operating even when the main players are in jail. They smuggle cell phones into jail, bribe guards, deliver personal messages through legitimate visitation, or any other creative ideas to keep the continuity of communication with the outside work and their organizations.

If this sounds like a business plan, then you understand the concept. Make no mistake, drug dealing is big business. The return on investment is massive. It's an evil business. It's a destructive business. Satan's favorite weapon is drugs, and they fit the pattern depicted in John 10:10 (KJV), *"The thief cometh not, but for to steal, and to kill and to destroy: I am come that they might have life, and that they might have it more abundantly."* Look carefully at the three stages revealed in this scripture. The first is stealing, then it's killing, and finally there's total destruction. Drugs will steal; drugs will kill, but drugs are never satisfied until they destroy their victim. Sounds a lot like our adversary, the devil. I did not know this seedy world even existed, and now as a drug agent my job was to try to stop it.

In the early fall of 1987 I witnessed my first drug deal. The transaction took place in a small community of approximately 5,000 people, in Marlow, Oklahoma. Our game plan was to conduct a "buy-walk" drug deal. A buy-walk is when you "buy" a quantity of drugs for a price and then you let your money "walk" away. In other words, you do not immediately arrest the defendant. The defendants have no idea their covert, illicit drug operation has been compromised. By not facilitating the arrest, the defendant gains confidence that you are not the police.

I observed as my Senior Agent and I met the confidential informant on a rural, dirt road outside of Marlow. We searched the confidential informant so we could testify that he did not have any controlled dangerous substances on him before the transaction took place. We did this to strengthen the credibility of the informant. A body transmitting device was placed on the confidential source to allow the surveillance team to monitor the transaction. Technology has advanced incredibly over the years, but in 1987 we had a very crude body microphone system. It was big, bulky, and very hard to conceal. In addition, the only way to attach the body microphone system to the body was duct tape. Duct tape is vicious when it comes to any hair on the body. It was torture! Not a hair removal procedure I would recommend. The one positive thing was once you duct taped it to your body, you never had to worry about the body microphone slipping because it was guaranteed to hang on.

I watched the confidential informant very closely and wondered how a person could get to this point in his life. Does a string of bad decisions land a person in jail, and then he tries to help himself by turning state's witness? Or as a confidential source, is he doing it to make money? Or is it to eliminate the competition? Even though these are a few motives, the reality is confidential sources could have any motive in the world to do what they do. I once had an informant that helped the police because the target was allegedly sexually molesting a family member. That is an honorable reason to want to secure a case on an offender and get him off the streets.

The confidential informant exited the vehicle and conducted a body microphone check, and we gave him a thumbs up. He was now walking toward the small neighborhood bar where he would attempt to purchase a gram of methamphetamine. The vocal sound quality produced via the crude body microphone was not very clear. Often we would hear a string of the conversation, and then the audio would go silent for several seconds, and then it would be clear again. It would pick up background noise and clothing rubbing up against the microphone. It was primitive at best, but the primary function of the body microphone transmitter was for the safety of the undercover whether he be an agent or a confidential informant.

Technology has since advanced, but at that time, it seemed state-of-the-art and we found a way to make it work. When you're on surveillance, you take notes and record times of different events as the drug deal progresses. What time did you start? What time did the undercover meet the target defendant? What significant conversation did we hear over the body transmitter while the undercover was meeting the target defendant? All of these were needed when the case was prosecuted and the defendant was brought to trial. We call it the not-so-fun stuff in narcotic enforcement.

More important than all of the note taking was listening for distress or possible problems the undercover may be having while attempting the drug transaction. We never know when the target is going to try to rob him or grab the money and run. Many small-time dealers also are heavy users, which amplifies the volatility of the transaction. Users are more dangerous dealers than the dealers who do not use. They can get big time crazy in a flash. We have to be prepared while conducting surveillance to act in a split second and go into rescue mode.

On this night, the little neighborhood bar was quiet, and background noise was not significant. We could hear as the confidential informant met the subject and called him by his first name. They had a brief conversation about the quality of the methamphetamine, and the dealer assured the confidential source that it was a high quality, and it would definitely get him off on an incredible high. This damaging evidence incriminated the defendant, and he would have a hard time in a court of law denying the methamphetamine deal. The confidential source then exited the bar and walked down the alley.

We could hear him breathing heavily and walking briskly toward our vehicle. We picked him up and drove to an off-site location away from town where we took custody of the small baggie of methamphetamine. We re-searched the confidential source, and no other drugs were found. We then removed the body transmitting microphone from the informant's body. The confidential source personally took the duct tape off, hair and all, along with maybe even a layer of flesh. Ouch! We then transported the confidential source to a secure location where we paid him a nominal amount of money. Many low-level informants work for small amounts of cash. He departed the area, and I never made another undercover deal with the informant.

I had just listened to my first drug deal, and all I could think about was, "Does this really go on in the world?" Here we were in a small rural community of 5,000 people on a back street, in a small bar, and a gram of methamphetamine was sold. If this was happening in this small community, how many more drug deals were being conducted in every community in Oklahoma? How many drug transactions were being conducted on dirt roads, alleyways, side streets, bars, and back rooms around our state? How many in the entire United States? How deep was the problem? Just maybe as a young agent, I did not need to know the answer to those questions as I would eventually learn firsthand. Oh, how I would learn! I was shocked by our society, but eventually nothing would shock me.

3

THE ROAD TRIP

All new agents are taught the three things that a drug agent must do to minimize the risks in a drug deal and undercover operation, although we never totally eliminate danger or the chance of something going bad. We strive to mitigate the risk as much as we can. The first thing we must remember in planning a drug deal is that we control the deal. The second thing that we must do is control the deal. I will let you guess the third element: We control the deal. Control in any type of dangerous situation, undercover transaction, or search warrant is vital. We must never let the target pick the location, time, or anything of substance when attempting to organize a drug deal.

When we stand for what is right, the evil in the world will always set out to destroy us. Throughout history, the Bible tells of encouraging stories of individuals doing what was right and God finding a way to rescue His servants when the enemy comes against them. God is in the rescue business. As an undercover agent, I often thought about Daniel Chapter 6, which told us a remarkable story of Daniel and King Darius. King Darius was persuaded to make a decree that no one was to offer prayer to any god except him for a time. However, Daniel stood for what was right and continued to pray to the true God knowing that praying would likely bring bodily harm to him. Darius had Daniel arrested and thrown into a lions' den and sealed the entrance. It looked like Daniel had zero chance of surviving. Daniel knew he would likely be crushed to death in seconds by the lions' powerful jaws.

The next morning, King Darius came to the lions' den to see if God had rescued Daniel. Daniel was found unharmed and reported that God sent an angel to shut the mouths of the lions. He was not hurt and was brought out of the den unscathed. The story of Daniel strengthened my faith as I prepared mentally, physically, and spiritually to enter into the lions' den of drug dealers. I believe that God never changes, and if He delivered Daniel, He would deliver Darrell. God is the same yesterday, today, and forever, and He would find an escape for me. Drug traffickers are very similar to the lions: They can bite, and when they bite it's very unforgiving.

I was fortunate as a junior narcotics agent that my first senior agent and training officer was Senior Agent Leroy Glass. Senior Agent Glass was a quiet, mild-mannered Native American who was very cautious in all of his actions. He was so quiet that rumor had it, in the past he had spent several weeks with a new junior agent, and he never spoke a word. Like the old saying goes, "Still waters run deep." In other words, a person's calm exterior sometimes conceals great depths of toughness and character. If that is the case, then Leroy was a mile and a half deep. Fortunately for me, Senior Agent Glass and I hit it off and quickly became close friends.

Senior Agent Glass was a very interesting individual. He was about 6 feet 1 inch tall and a lean 190 pounds. He trained in aikido. Aikido is a Japanese martial art that practitioners can use to defend themselves while also protecting their attacker from injury. It redirects the momentum of an opponent's attack. Aikido always seemed to be a flowing martial art, and Senior Agent Glass was very much graceful like aikido. He was soft-spoken, and his physical being had an aura that seemed to flow. However, he had an intense side to him and a reputation as someone who would pull the trigger and shoot! He wasn't afraid to mix it up. Senior Agent Glass had been involved in several shootings at the agency during his very short tenure.

One of his shootings was during the investigation of a cultivated marijuana field where an individual was growing smoke. A team of agents led by Senior Agent Glass captured the suspect, but it wasn't without drama. During the facilitation of the arrest, the individual pointed a gun at the officers, and Senior Agent Glass shot the perpetrator with a shotgun. Miraculously, the individual survived the shooting. When the arrest team drew their weapons and attempted the arrest, they yelled, "State Police!!" It happened in the fall, so the bad guy claimed he did not know they were police, and said the agents screamed, "Trick or Treat!" Yeah right. That argument wasn't very compelling in a court of law.

Another of Senior Agent Glass' shootings happened in a restaurant parking lot. He finished his meal and walked outside when he noticed an individual was stealing from patrons' vehicles while they ate. Senior Agent Glass attempted to stop him. The individual jumped into a getaway vehicle and was believed to have displayed a weapon. Feeling his life was threatened, Senior Agent Glass shot at the bad guy and ended up blowing the back car window out. Some people have an after-meal mint; he preferred slinging lead down range at car thieves. The suspect was never caught as he sped away across a vacant field; however, the muddy tires' tracks were a short-lived monument of what happens when crossing Senior Agent Glass.

In the dangerous world of drug enforcement and as a junior agent, I always felt safe when Senior Agent Glass was with me. I had a secure feeling knowing the agents on surveillance had my back, and they would come with guns blazing if needed. Senior Agent Glass had proven he would do just that and wasn't afraid to take action. Since he had been in so many violent encounters, he was always overly cautious, and that is not a bad thing in drug enforcement. He always moved slowly and very methodically. It made me think in a very strategic way, and I always built in contingency plans. I had to learn this concept early in my career, and no experience made this clearer than the time I fondly remember as "the trip."

An undercover agent begins his career by doing hand-to-hand buys. The hand-to-hand buys are drug transactions in which the undercover police officer is actually adopting a temporary, new identity while purchasing the drugs from the bad guy. Obviously, it would be impossible to go undercover and tell them you are a police officer, and would you please sell me drugs so I can send you to jail? It doesn't work that way. A good undercover officer must be quick on his feet and possess strong courage, boldness, and a healthy control of fear. Sometimes a confidential informant is involved, but the objective is the officer exchanges the money and drugs personally. This type of deal provides several advantages. The most important is it produces a much stronger case in the courtroom when prosecuting the case. The officer's credibility is much less likely to be questioned than a confidential informant's.

We learn that we can never force a drug deal, but young agents want the transactions to go, and the desire to make a case on the defendant is sometimes overwhelming. However, we can never give up safety for a drug deal. It is not worth the risk. An old drug enforcement saying is, "The bad guy can be caught on another day." Rarely in my career did I ever see a legitimate bad guy not "catch a case" in his lifetime. They try to insulate themselves, but they all can be caught.

We had a target that through a confidential informant agreed to meet and sell methamphetamine at a location we called Biscuit Hill in Caddo County. This location was pretty much in the middle of nowhere. I made an undercover telephone call with the seller, but he was unable to meet me that evening.

The following day, we attempted to make contact again telephonically to arrange the transaction. We left a message and waited for his return call. While we were waiting, my Agent-in-Charge, Jim Henry, started showing me autopsy pictures of an individual who was killed by law enforcement during a shootout in Garfield County many years ago. Agent-in-Charge Henry was involved in the shootout and started telling the facts of the case.

The Sheriff had an arrest warrant for a perpetrator, so he and local deputies went to the man's residence in rural Garfield County to facilitate the arrest. When they arrived at the residence, they went in and were met by a hail of gunfire. Several of the lawmen were seriously injured, and the assailant fled into the woods. Law enforcement came from all over the state to assist. A very dangerous person was unaccounted for and needed to be caught. The Bureau of Narcotics responded to help in the man hunt.

A security perimeter was set up within a one-mile area. Law enforcement felt confident the shooter was within the one square mile, but there was a problem—a huge problem. In the daylight, monitoring the roads was easy, but the task was much more difficult in darkness, and darkness was looming. If he wasn't caught before sundown, then he would surely escape covertly and possibly go commit other crimes while on the run. He needed to be caught now.

They had to get a team together to go in after him. The mission would be dangerous as the land was flat with very few trees. The area did not have much cover or concealment. To make matters worse, they knew the bad guy was armed. So they hastily searched for volunteers to form a team. Eventually several Oklahoma Bureau of Narcotics agents bravely volunteered along with only one other local police officer. Many officers were out there, but not many hands were raised to volunteer for such peril.

The team gathered up their weapons and started walking through the open field. They would cautiously take every step not knowing when he would pop up out of one of the small ravines. Each step could be their last step. An aircraft was launched above trying to spot him from the air. Then in a split second the agents caught something out of the corners of their eyes. The bad guy had his dog with him and they spotted the dog's movement. The bad guy was crouched beside the dog and was looking up at the airplane. At that moment, he spotted the agents and lowered his rifle to shoot. Fortunately, the agents had the split-second notice and jumped out of the bullets' way as they zipped by them, barely missing one agent. The agents then returned fire with a volley of shots killing the bad guy and his dog.

Death had come to this individual. He now transcended into eternity. To pass judgment on his soul at that moment would be easy. He obviously had made horrible decisions, but I refused to play God. Matthew 7:1-2 (KJV) says, *"Judge not, that ye be not judged. For with what judgment ye judge, ye shall be judged: and with what measure ye mete, it shall be measured to you again."* I elected not to judge him, but to learn from him. I wanted to stay alive, and this was serious business. The timing of looking at the autopsy pictures made me very edgy, and it increased my determination not to let a defendant kill me in this job. The photographs were a reflection of an obviously violent encounter, but they made me more determined. The old saying that a picture is worth a thousand words was so real that night. I had seen dead bodies before, but not one with multiple bullet holes. It was an eye opener.

Finally in the latter part of the week we made contact telephonically with the defendant, and this time he agreed to meet and sell me methamphetamine. The surveillance team was made up of Senior Agent Glass and only one other agent. The surveillance team was anemic with only two agents, so Senior Agent Glass clearly gave me instructions to meet the target at Biscuit Hill and make the transaction. He then directed me under no circumstances was I to travel with the defendant to a second location. In the drug world, when you travel with the defendant to the second location this is commonly known as "tripping" with the target. As a junior agent, we never want to trip because you never know where you are going to end up, and it's very difficult for a small surveillance team to keep up with you in an undercover capacity without being detected.

The undercover agent is generally more comfortable than the surveillance team. As an undercover agent you obviously are the one observing the defendant and watching his nonverbal and verbal communication being displayed to you. In other words, you are in control. He may have thought the priority was the transaction, but little did he know that was not my main objective. My main priority was to stay alive and come out of the deal unharmed. Buying the dope was secondary. At 6 feet 1 inch tall and 190 pounds, I was always in good shape and trained hard to obtain a physical edge against the bad guys. I had to be careful because in my mind I became nine feet tall and bulletproof. I was asked several times, "Did you ever get scared undercover?" I think everyone gets a little scared, but I always turned the fear into a heightened sense of awareness of my surroundings. It is interesting how focused you are on every detail of an event if you think a person might try to kill you. It quickly changes the playing field.

Being on surveillance is totally the opposite of being the undercover agent. Whereas the undercover has a high degree of control and immediate awareness over the deal, the surveillance has little control or knowledge. They have to keep up with the movement of the deal, even though they do not know what will change in the next ten seconds of an extremely fluid situation. All of this must happen without being detected by the perpetrator. Surveillance is listening over some type of audio transmitting device, and often distinguishing what is being said is difficult. Maybe worse, they are not able to witness firsthand the non-verbal communication of the defendant, which often reveals more significant information than what is being said.

The surveillance agents can only listen closely and attempt—through the words used by the undercover or by inflection of voices—to determine if the undercover agent is in distress. All undercover transactions have an operation plan that is briefed before every enforcement action. This plan details everyone's responsibilities before, during, and after the deal has been made. Every attempt is made by the entire team to stick with the plan, especially the undercover operative.

However, situations sometimes arise, and you have to change the original plan. You never intentionally change because the surveillance team may not hear your signal and may be unaware of the change. Many times you have to make a slight, incremental change while on the move during the deal. As an undercover agent, you always desire trustworthy, focused agents on surveillance who have your safety at the top of their priority list for the day. You sure do not want your surveillance team in some fog with their minds a million miles away while you're trying to fight for your life with some bad guy undercover.

Remember I mentioned above, one of the cardinal rules of undercover is that you do not leave the original location and travel to another location unless it is clearly part of your operation plan. If you are to meet in the parking lot of a convenience store, then that's where you stay; you do not leave and go to a second location.

I met the defendant on Biscuit Hill and had a brief conversation concerning my methamphetamine purchase. We decided to load up in my vehicle and travel a short distance to obtain the methamphetamine. I was very confident with this guy, and I was not worried about anything going bad. It was a temporary lapse in judgement because the team was not prepared for travel. I was like a kid who did not pay attention to his parents and immediately did what I was not supposed to do. Like the typical drug dealer, he didn't tell me the entire truth. That is no surprise. Drug dealers lie. He then told me that there was another location only a few miles away. Because of my inexperience, I continued to drive. Let the goose chase begin. Poor surveillance team, will they ever forgive me?

I was planning what I would do physically if the defendant elected to attack me or attempted some type of robbery. I did not even think about the fact that the surveillance team was trying desperately to keep up with me. They were in a panic! I never gave verbal signals over the audio transmitter about direction of travel or landmarks to make their job easier. I was so comfortable that it didn't cross my mind. Not good. Later I would learn how easy it was to verbally identify landmarks in your undercover conversation as you passed them, covertly notifying surveillance of your location. They were scrambling to keep me in their sights, and by a miracle they did not lose me. The undercover officer always feels much more confident than the surveillance agents. I learned later they were in a high state of anxiety trying to keep up, yet I was enjoying an uneventful drive through beautiful, rural Oklahoma. I felt in complete control, nine feet tall and bulletproof, as the miles rolled by my window.

Eventually, I realized that approximately an hour had passed and I was still with this clown. My how time flies when you are having fun! Only the vehicle's odometer would be able to testify how many miles we had driven. I am glad I started with a full tank of gas! We ended up in the middle of nowhere. A little sparse community of a few houses that was not even large enough to have a name. It then dawned on me: We were just driving in obscurity. At that point, I started getting suspicious of the defendant. Something started to feel wrong. I got the feeling he was not able to get me the dope, but even worse, I began to think he may try to rob me.

I started formulating an exit strategy out of this eternal, infinite drug deal. The more I tried to think, the more the bad guy was talking. He was talking so loud and fast and was really getting on my nerves. Based on my conversation, I soon realized that he was not a significant drug dealer and was just an addict looking to score some drugs for himself. So how was I going to get this guy out of my car? He acted like he wanted to be a permanent fixture as shotgun in my vehicle, and that was not going to happen. I decided it was time for the dude to leave.

I could see a large farmhouse on a hill about two miles away. It was the typical Oklahoma country home, an old, two-story frame house with several outbuildings and small barns in the backyard. We drove past the house, and he told me to turn around. So I turned the vehicle around and made my way back toward the old farmhouse. He then asked me to turn into the driveway, which circled around the back of the house. As I pulled up into the driveway, I observed Senior Agent Glass and the surveillance team driving down the road. Praise God, they did not lose me.

As we slowly drove to the back of the house, a pickup truck with an unidentified male, driving erratically, pulled into the back yard. His body was bobbing up and down as he hit ruts in the back yard. He rolled down his window and frantically told the target that there were people driving around everywhere! He insisted that something was going on, and he was nervous. Oh my, at that point I knew that the surveillance had been spotted and that I needed to get out of there as soon as possible. I brought my vehicle to a complete stop, but I kept it in gear looking for the window of opportunity to escape. The defendant then opened the passenger-side door and told me it's too risky. He instructed me to come into the house. He was in panic mode and started to freak out. His eyes were jerking from side to side. He was getting more unpredictable every second. I told him it was too treacherous to go into his house, and I just wanted to get out of there, but he continued to argue with me and insisted I come into the house. Little did he know that there was zero chance I was going to get out of that car and go into that residence with him! Finally, the bad guy got out of the car and ran to the house. The door was not even closed as I seized the opportunity and hammered the accelerator. The passenger-side door slammed shut on its own as I expeditiously drove over the ruts. Mud and dirt were flying through the backyard as I made my way to the country road. My head was bobbing up and down, and I felt like a bobble doll. I was going so fast, and there was so much dust in the air, it looked like an F-3 tornado had just hit.

I drove several miles away from the house and then pulled over to talk personally to the surveillance team. I could immediately tell Senior Agent Glass was extremely upset. I had never seen him mad as it was way out of character for him. He in no uncertain terms told me to get to the office. I started to drive toward the office, and it was then that I realized I was in a totally different county than where I began. As I traveled back to Lawton, crisscrossing through the back roads to find a main highway, a cold chill ran down my spine because I realized just how far I had traveled passing through multiple counties. This was not good, and I knew I was in a heap of trouble.

We made it back to the Lawton district office. Senior Agent Glass and I met in the small conference room in the back of the office. The long ride back had not been very successful at calming him down, and he was still very upset. We were nose to nose and at this point, both of us very angry, upset, and tired. It was escalating into an unpleasant situation with 6 feet 1 inch, 190 pound aikido master Senior Agent Leroy Glass on one side and 6 feet 1 inch, 190 pound taekwondo power lifter Junior Agent Weaver on the other side, and we were about to come to blows. This was not going to be pretty for either party involved. Even the loser was going to come out of this with at least a broken jaw. That was the minimum damage expected if we were to come to blows.

Thank goodness calmer heads prevailed, and no blows were thrown. He let me have it verbally with both barrels and communicated how I had placed the surveillance team in a troubling situation by taking such a long road trip over three counties. As a junior narcotics undercover agent, I had felt totally in control but quickly realized that I had not done my partners right, and I had let the dealer call the shots.

Senior Agent Glass was right: I had screwed up. I was fortunate and blessed that nothing bad happened to me or the surveillance team, and truly the whole road trip was out of control. In the future, many of my under-cover experiences ended up being much more dangerous than this road trip, but this deal was a valuable learning tool about not taking chances and how quickly you can drift away from the original plan and get yourself into a bind. I vowed that this lack of control over a drug deal would never happen again to me in my career, and it never did. You have to control everything, and I had inadvertently lost control.

I also had a valuable lesson on wisdom. Wisdom in its simplest form is a maturation of life that causes you to develop a body of knowledge and display good judgement. I realized I needed wisdom to survive in the world of narcotic enforcement. Proverbs 4:7 (NIV) says, *"The beginning of wisdom is this: Get wisdom. Though it cost all you have, get understanding."* I had to listen closer to my senior agents or it was going to cost me the ultimate price, and that was my life.

4

MACHINE GUN VS. COCAINE

Three components are common in most undercover drug transactions. They are drugs, money, and guns. Normally, drugs are being supplied by the source, money is given as in any type of purchase of a commodity, and guns are brought to the transaction for protection of the players. Every undercover police officer believes that the drug trafficker has a weapon or there is a weapon in close proximity of where they are located. The drug trade is so dangerous and violent that guns are a must and very commonplace.

I recall a time while I was undercover in an apartment complex in Duncan, Oklahoma. I had purchased methamphetamine several times from an individual who worked as a maintenance man at another apartment complex in Duncan. The confidential informant had told me that the target was mild mannered, and it would be an easy transaction. Any time an informant tells you something is going to be easy then you better get ready, something is about to happen, and it usually is not good. On this particular day, we went to the defendant's apartment, which was on a second floor of the complex. The informant and I met him around noon while he was having lunch.

As a defensive tactics instructor, I taught undercover survival techniques and always thought tactically while undercover and methodically planned on how I could survive in case of a violent encounter. I was pretty confident of the deal, but I always proceed with caution. My informant was a very trusted former all-state basketball player who stood about 6 feet 7 inches, had a charismatic personality, and could talk his way out of anything. He was a charmer with a million dollar smile and could sell snow to an Eskimo. I called him, "Mack."

We entered the tiny apartment. It was no more than a few hundred square feet in the combined living and dining area. The defendant was sitting on the couch eating a sandwich in the living room. He was watching TV with his back to us. His girlfriend was in the kitchen area banging on pots and pans. I was in the perfect tactical position. After our initial greetings, I told him I wanted an "eight ball" of methamphetamine. An eight ball was the slang term for one-eighth of an ounce quantity, which was a common amount bought by average users. His girlfriend walked out of the room toward the back of the apartment to retrieve the dope. As she exited, the defendant leaned back on the couch with his back to us. He was still watching TV and placed his hand on the back of the couch. I was standing behind the defendant. The confidential informant was standing beside me. In a blink of an eye, and I do mean very rapidly, the defendant reached back and flipped up my shirt. It literally happened within a split second, and I could not stop it. I carried a five shot .38 caliber undercover revolver in my front waistband so I could get to it quickly if needed. When the defendant flipped my shirt up, he immediately saw the gun. His girlfriend was walking back into the room and also saw it and screamed, "He has a gun!!"

It got intense quick! For a moment, I was on edge wondering what was going to happen next. The surveillance team outside was scrambling thinking that there was soon to be a shootout, or they would have to come rescue me. One agent was snacking on potato chips, and he flung the bag in a near panic. The confidential informant said in a very calm manner, "Everyone carries a gun on a dope deal." The defendant seemed to agree, but his girlfriend was acting goofy and made me uneasy. I still didn't know if the revelation of the gun was going to send the deal into a violent encounter.

What the bad guy did not realize was that Mack was closer to him than I was, and he was wearing what the defendant was searching for, the body wire. We would have easily been compromised if he would've only picked the shirt of the other person.

We had another issue. The defendant did not have the right change for the transaction. He got up from the couch and walked out of our sight into a back bedroom. This made me very nervous because I did not know if he would come around the corner with a gun. I was already planning and thinking, "What would I do next if he came out suddenly with a gun?" I quickly decided that if he came back brandishing a weapon, I was going to dive over the couch for cover in a diversionary maneuver while pulling my weapon. I would try to get off a round or make him miss his shot. It was a tense 45 seconds as we waited for him to come back into the room. Finally, he turned the corner with only change in his hand, and I was relieved. He gave me the money, and we exited the apartment.

God protected us, again. A split-second decision could have caused an escalation of force or a life or death situation. He saw me in that apartment complex and was with me. Joshua 1:9 (NIV) says, *"Have I not commanded you? Be strong and courageous. Do not be afraid; do not be discouraged, for the Lord your God will be with you wherever you go."*

As Mack and I made our way to the vehicle, we discussed the incident. He disclosed to me that previously when he was there alone with the defendant that he had searched him trying to locate a body wire. I couldn't believe that Mack had not shared this with me! This knowledge would have put me on high alert, and we would have thought through more carefully where the body wire was placed. It only showed me again that you can never fully trust informants. He was a good confidential informant and did a lot of cases for me. We eventually went undercover many times and had high levels of success, but you could never fully trust an informant, including him.

Guns were common in any drug deal—a piece of the puzzle that was an almost guarantee. As Christians, our weapon and sword is God's Word. We must take that word in our hearts with us. The drug dealer will not conduct a drug transaction without a gun, and I was not going to do a drug transaction without the most important weapon, and that is God's Word hidden in my heart. Not everyone has a dangerous profession where guns may be drawn on a daily basis, but as Christians, all of us have battles every day, and all of us have adversaries. We should never approach our jobs, our families' challenges, and circumstances without our most critical weapon. That weapon is the Word of God.

My next undercover transaction would not simply be someone brandishing a gun, but the whole transaction would be driven by the purchase of a fully automatic weapon! I was contacted by federal agents and local law enforcement in Washita County about an individual named Sean Evans, who law enforcement believed to be heavily involved in cocaine and other controlled dangerous substances. Even more troubling was local law enforcement believed that Evans was involved in a murder at Foss Lake. Intelligence information indicated that Evans prided himself on being a "ninja warrior" type and was a suspect in the beating death of an individual found at the lake.

I was not aware of Evans mainly because he resided in a very small community of Carter, Oklahoma, which was several miles from my home duty station. Oklahoma only has 3.8 million people with two major metro areas, Oklahoma City and Tulsa. Several towns are midsize, but most of Oklahoma is made up of small communities with very small populations. Carter, Oklahoma, was one such community with a population of 273 people. Not even one signal light in the entire town. However, being a small town does not eliminate it from having criminal behavior. Many times the drug dealers will gravitate to small communities because of the limited law enforcement presence and resources. They think they can hide and not be detected.

Commonly, local law enforcement will seek out the Oklahoma Bureau of Narcotics agents to go undercover because not all law enforcement agencies have covert operatives. As a matter of fact, they are very rare. I was once told by a friend who was a patrol officer from a major state patrol agency that he could never entertain going undercover because it is such a dangerous role, and you lose your identity as a law enforcement officer. You have no uniform or visible badge for people to realize that you are the authority figure. When you're undercover you assume the role of the bad guy, and most law enforcement personnel do not have a desire for such a shift from normal police work. It's understandable. Obviously, all law enforcement have dangerous situations, and stopping vehicles on traffic stops without knowing who you are about to come into contact with at that moment can quickly bring great peril. It all takes courage.

We travelled to Washita County to meet and get details concerning Evans. At the meeting, I was informed that Evans told their informant that he had a fully automatic machine gun that he would trade for a quantity of powdered cocaine. The law enforcement in the area believed that Evans was capable of owning or having access to a fully automatic machine gun. They wanted me to go undercover on Evans and do a "reverse" sting operation where I would provide the cocaine and Evans would supply the fully automatic machine gun. Also, they wanted me to attempt to solicit information concerning Evan's involvement in the Foss Lake murder. He was the prime suspect in the homicide.

Reverse operations are highly dangerous, and an additional level of control must be inserted. Normally, law enforcement provides money to purchase drugs and can allow the money to walk. In other words, allow the defendant to actually keep the money. In a reverse operation, law enforcement provides and exchanges something that they cannot allow on the streets. Sometimes it is large quantities of drugs that the drug distributor wants for resale. In return, they supply the money. Obviously, law enforcement cannot allow those drugs onto the street.

In this circumstance, we would provide Evans an ounce of powdered cocaine in a barter or exchange with him for the fully automatic machine gun. So control of the transaction would be of utmost importance. We cannot allow the cocaine to leave our sight, and Evans must be arrested immediately upon the exchange of goods.

This was exactly the kind of challenge a young narcotics agent thrived on, and it got my adrenaline pumping. Remember, when we are undercover we feel nine feet tall and bulletproof. One must have a high-level of courage and when this courage is activated, the body has an adrenaline rush. To go undercover and take Evans off the street and possibly solve a murder would be great! I was all in on the deal.

Evans had a reputation as being absolutely nuts and extremely dangerous. I couldn't think or dwell on his crazy reputation because it would bring about fear. I didn't have time for fear; all I could think about was bringing him to justice. I had to get him off the streets. An additional risk in an undercover operation is that when you're undercover you seldom wear a bulletproof vest. Vests are often bulky and hard to conceal. The bad guy would recognize it immediately and thus reveal your identity as a police officer. Without a vest, you are vulnerable to knives, clubs, or bullets, unlike any other time in our profession. Therefore, being undercover could be argued as the most dangerous moment in the law enforcement profession. This risk is embraced by the undercover officer, but it also enhances the officer's awareness because he or she must eliminate the possibility of a mistake.

I met with the confidential informant, briefed him on how we wanted to conduct the transaction, and made our original phone call to Evans. The call went extremely well, and Evans seemed anxious and was insistent that he was able to deliver a fully automatic machine gun. In my mind, I questioned why he trusted me so quickly, but a lot of his trust had to do with the fact that he had a high level of trust in the informant. Often, you're only as strong undercover as your informant.

I talked to Evans telephonically several times, and each time I told him my reason for needing to obtain the machine gun was to make a professional hit. We discussed my desire to do a contract killing. Being a hitman was the undercover role that I had assumed, and I believed it would put Evans at ease. I was hopeful that he would start talking about the murder he was suspected of doing. Evans and I seemed to be communicating well, and it was getting close to the time for a personal meeting. However, I never could get him to talk about the Foss Lake murder. My plan was to bring the killing up in a conversation with him when we met and made the exchange.

I started the process of obtaining the powdered cocaine, which I would use in the barter for the fully automatic machine gun. The Director of the Oklahoma Bureau of Narcotics is the only person in the state of Oklahoma who can authorize any individual to lawfully hold narcotics or drugs. So any time law enforcement wants to do a reverse sting operation and utilize a controlled dangerous substance like cocaine in a transaction, that law enforcement officer must get written approval from the Director to obtain those drugs.

The procedure is easy, and key elements must be included in the request letter such as, who is responsible for the drugs? Where will the drugs be stored when not being utilized? What is the timeframe of the undercover operation? By what date will the drugs be submitted back to the laboratory for testing? These are the elements that all officers must submit or they cannot do the transaction, and the Oklahoma Bureau of Narcotics agents are no different. Even though we work for the same agency and were commissioned by the Director, we still had to go through the same procedure.

I supplied the request letter through my chain of command, the Director signed off on it, and I took possession of one ounce of powdered cocaine to conduct the transaction with Evans. Even though I was in lawful possession of cocaine, it made me feel funny to have it and, frankly, a little bit nervous. I secured the cocaine in our office safe until the day came when I needed to conduct the transaction.

Through a series of negotiations with Evans, we decided that we would meet around 2 o'clock at the convenience store in Carter, Oklahoma. You have to remember that Carter only had a population of approximately 300 people and had only one convenience store. It was in August, and Oklahoma can get very warm with temperatures many days exceeding

100°F. This day was no different, and it started out a hot, muggy day. The surveillance team met that morning and formulated a game plan. Surveillance could get tricky in such a small town where everyone knows everyone. Our main focus was that Evans was in no way going to leave the premises with the cocaine; controlling him would be critical to our success. After I obtain possession of the fully automatic machine gun, I would then hand the cocaine to Evans and immediately facilitate the arrest. I knew at that moment it was going to be a dangerous situation, but I was prepared mentally and physically, and most importantly spiritually, to achieve the mission. At the end of the day, Evans had to be in custody and off the street.

I noticed in the briefing how many people and different agencies were present to help. We had to have superior forces on surveillance because keeping a covert presence without being detected was going to be a challenge. The local residents know who drives a specific type of vehicle, and they are always suspicious when they don't recognize an individual in their community. Not to mention, many Oklahomans in small communities are related to each other, so it multiplies the mistrust of strangers. We weren't sure who was related to Evans and how many eyes would be conducting counter surveillance for him.

I agreed to meet Evans at the convenience store. We planned I would "flash him" or momentarily show him the cocaine, but in no way would I hand him the cocaine without having the machine gun. So I arrived at the store and waited for Evans. I was parked to the left of the store almost on the side of the building. The surveillance team was watching and trying to maintain their covert status. I had never met Evans before, but had numerous pictures of him. I would be able to recognize him on the spot. My head was on a swivel as I watched everything around me.

Eventually, I observed an individual walking toward my vehicle, and I immediately realized it was Evans. The deal was on, and my adrenaline started to pump. Evans came to the vehicle, opened the door, and sat down in the front seat beside me. I asked him where the machine gun was and he said he had it, but would have to put it together. He asked if I had the cocaine. I told him that I had the cocaine, but I was not giving it to him until I had the machine gun. He appeared anxious. It was a tense moment. At that critical point, I knew I had to control the situation, or the bad guy would believe that he could get the upper hand. It could be deadly if I lost control of the deal.

I wanted to bring up the killing at Foss Lake but things were happening too rapidly, and all I could think about was to control the moment. He finally told me that he would go get the machine gun, reassemble it, and bring it back to me. I told him that I didn't want a piece of junk that would not shoot properly, and it better be fully automatic. Evans assured me that it was a fully automatic and a functional weapon, then he left my vehicle.

I drove from the store and made my way slowly around the block. I had a covert handheld walkie-talkie, and I communicated to the surveillance team what was going on with Evans. They reported they could hear the body transmitter clear and were aware of what was going on. They were immensely concerned about how long they could continue to conduct surveillance.

I returned back to the small convenience store and waited on Evans to return. Eventually, I could see him walking toward my vehicle. This time he had a brown sack in his hands. It looked promising. I started to gain confidence he really had the machine gun. However, this time Evans threw me a curveball. Instead of getting in the front seat, he got in the back seat behind me! This was not good. We are trained from the very beginning of undercover operations you never put a bad guy behind you. I immediately jumped to code red in my internal awareness. I should have locked the back doors! He out maneuvered me for the moment.

Evans again seemed very skittish. He actually stated that he felt like there were cops everywhere and noticed several vehicles around town that he didn't recognize. He could sense something was not right. I knew that this situation could turn bad in a split second. Here we were in an undercover transaction, I had an ounce of powdered cocaine, the bad guy had a fully automatic machine gun, and now he is starting to act crazy! Not a prescription for a pleasant day.

Evans was now talking fast, and I could barely understand him. He wanted to see the cocaine, but I stuck to my guns and insisted I see the machine gun first. He then pulled a gun out of the brown sack. It appeared to be some type of foreign-made submachine gun with a pistol grip and a short barrel. I had a random thought and said to myself, "This stuff is what movies are made out of." I asked him if it was fully automatic and he said, "Yes, and I have fired it, and it shot well." I then started a conversation about trying to do a contract murder, but Evans would not talk about anything of that nature. He insisted on seeing the cocaine. I then reached under the seat, retrieved the ounce of powdered cocaine, and handed it to Evans.

It was amazing what I witnessed in Evans' eyes. Matthew 6:22 (NIV) talks about the eyes are the window of the soul. It says, *"The eye is the lamp of the body. If your eyes are healthy, your whole body will be full of light."* I saw in Evans' eyes a look that appeared to be not only lustful, but evil. One glimpse of him looking at the cocaine triggered his addiction and his mouth started to drool. He was literally slobbering. I was caught up in witnessing firsthand the effect of addiction and how the body reacts. It was an ugly but powerful transformation. It was in the mind but gravitated to his whole body. It almost made him unhuman.

As planned, I had given the cocaine to Evans. It was evident that he had a plan too. As soon as he took possession of the cocaine, he was going to get the heck out of there. He had flight on his mind. He immediately opened the door and was outside my vehicle! Things were happening at warp speed. He was quick and was adhering to his plan. At that time I was carrying a large .357 Smith and Wesson revolver. It was a bulky, hog of a gun, but in this dangerous situation, I wanted as much firepower as I could carry. Evans was too dangerous for anything less.

I quickly pulled my revolver, opened the car door, and took cover in a tactical position behind the door. I had the vehicle between Evans and me. He had shorts on and no shirt, which was a big advantage to me as I was very confident he did not have a weapon. I would be able to see one if he had one. I shouted at Evans, "State Police don't move!" With the cocaine in his hand, he took off running like a rocket, crossing in front of my vehicle directly in front of me.

As fate would have it, two teenage kids walked out of the grocery store at that moment between Evans and me! It's funny how your surroundings slow down in dangerous situations. I knew I could not shoot because of the crossfire situation with the kids. I could not risk hitting the young people with a stray bullet. Evans did not seem to have an interest in fighting, but just to run, and man could he run. The dude should have been running track for the U.S. Olympic team!

I gave running chase to Evans and was screaming commands to halt, but it didn't seem like he had any interest in stopping and obeying. The race was on! I was in excellent shape, but there's nothing like running while carrying a big frame .357! It was like carrying a 50 pound dumbbell, but I continued the chase. Evans started running across a watermelon patch so now we had obstacles to avoid. We zigged and zagged through the watermelon patch. It would have been comical if it weren't so darn serious. I could see people giving chase from other parts of the field, and I could hear the revving of engines in the background. I was very confident that Carter, Oklahoma, was seeing more action than they'd ever seen. Surveillance was on the move, and now we had to somehow surround and capture Evans to place him under arrest.

Eventually after about a mile, Evans seemed to tire, and he stopped running. He was now walking very slowly and had the appearance of being winded. Maybe he should have worked more on cardio and less on weights. Commands were given to him to place his hands in the air and to get down on his knees. The closest agents were approximately 20 yards from him. Everything had stopped, and the race had been suspended; we were now hopeful for compliance. He seemed like he was ready to give up and placed his hands in the air and slowly started getting on his knees as he had his back to us. We then learned he had not given up! Evans was just biding time to rest as he then got into track starter stance and he was off again, running with a second wind and apparently a new sense of freedom.

So here we go again through the watermelon patch chasing him on the second leg of what seemed to be an eternal marathon. Eventually, Evans began getting tired again, and this time we could tell that we were closing in on him. He eventually stopped and got down on his knees as instructed. The race was nearly over but we were not going to rest just yet, not until he was cuffed. As we reached him, he was huffing and puffing. We secured handcuffs on him and placed him under arrest. I guess he decided that sitting in jail would be less strenuous than trying to outrun the State Narcotics Bureau.

When we caught him, to our surprise, Evans did not have the cocaine on him! My heart sank. Now we had to backtrack to see if we could locate where he had thrown it. We were confident he never made contact with anyone nor was he ever out of our sight, so it had to have been tossed along his path of escape. We swarmed the area, and I was very confident that we would find it, but still was nervous that we didn't have it in our possession. After searching, we located the bag in the watermelon patch about 200 meters behind Evans, and all of the cocaine was intact. I was relieved! Thank you Jesus! Evans was then carted off to jail. We interviewed him and drilled down on the Foss Lake killing, but could never get him to admit his involvement in the murder. I always felt we missed out on solving a murder, but it was not meant to be at this time.

The case was filed in federal court in the Western District in Oklahoma City. The federal system is a great place to file such cases because it was a firearms case in a drug deal which has enhanced penalties in the federal system. The feds would only take a few cases, but were very interested in this case because of the violent nature and past history of Evans.

One key component of the case was the fact that Evans presented himself as a distributor of a fully automatic weapon, and the prosecutors wanted me to verify whether or not the gun was fully automatic. So, we took the machine gun to a firing range, and I shot it. I was shocked I had the strength to pull the trigger to test fire the weapon because I learned the hard way that running a mile with a .357 magnum in your hand will make the wrist extremely sore. Honestly, it nearly crippled my ability to grip for a week.

Firing the rapid-fire gun was fun and appealed to the gun nut in me. It was hard to believe I got paid to do these types of things. The gun was fully automatic and fired very well. It could spit out a lot of rounds at one time.

I could not help but think, "What if this gun were in the wrong hands?" It reinforced how important it was to take the machine gun out of the hands of a wacko like Evans.

If ever there was a case in my career when I looked inside the destruction of addiction in the drug world I saw it that day when I looked into the eyes of Evans. It was a battle for a man's soul and a battle between the devil and his products of destruction. I saw it that day in the sleepy, quiet town of Carter, Oklahoma.

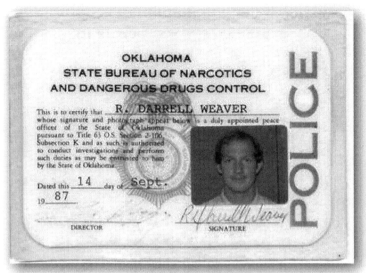

My first commission card at the bureau

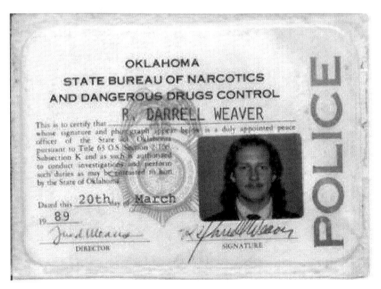

The commission card I carried during
many of my undercover drug deals

In a marijuana field with my faithful machine gun

Aerial view of a massive marijuana patch
in southeast Oklahoma

Darrell Weaver, David Taylor, and Gary Stoops at a marijuana eradication mission in Idabel, Oklahoma

Sparring for my black belt in Norman, Oklahoma

Goofy bicep pose taken at Camp Gruber
training facility in Braggs, Oklahoma

Surveillance on a marijuana field afforded a
great time to catch up on my reading

The team ready to make entry and safely secure a
residence and take contraband off the streets

Speaking on the south steps of the Oklahoma
State Capitol as agency Director in 2014

5

BAKER P. ROBERSON: CHAOS

Drug crimes are unique compared to other crimes in many ways. One unique feature of drug enforcement is that a drug deal is an in-progress crime. In other words, most crimes are investigated after the fact. You have an officer or investigator respond to the crime after the crime has been perpetrated. For example, in a homicide you have a body, and you work backwards to solve the crime. Most law enforcement falls into this type of category. Drug enforcement happens during the infiltration of the actual crime itself. If a person is cultivating marijuana, then it's in-progress because they are actually working the crops. If an individual is doctor shopping and scamming physicians for prescription drugs, then it is in-progress, and real people are involved. However, no example is more real than the actual undercover agent purchasing a quantity of drugs from a drug dealer. It does not get more in-progress than the undercover or UC deal.

Drug enforcement has another unique feature: the struggle with jurisdictional boundaries. Although not impossible, only in extremely rare cases does a drug dealer sell to someone who lives in the same residence; more commonly, the drug dealer sells to individuals in other locations. The drug traffickers' clientele could be across the street, on the other side of town, in a neighboring county, or even in another state—not to mention tribal lands. That is why one of the characteristic traits of a narcotics agent is the ability to have cordial relationships with law enforcement partners. Almost every case that the investigator works ends up crossing jurisdictional lines with other agencies and departments.

As Oklahoma Bureau of Narcotics Agents, we enjoyed the luxury of statewide jurisdiction and could investigate any drug crime and enforce actions within all 77 counties of our state. In addition, we had original jurisdiction, which meant we could conduct any drug investigation without being asked or invited by another law enforcement agency or department. This allowed the agency the ability to operate in a covert manner without the requirement of notification of local law enforcement. The special power was given in an attempt to keep the drug investigations quiet and without the possibility of compromise in communities. The problem was that if you do not work in cooperation with local law enforcement, then they begin to despise state law enforcement and the fact that you came into their jurisdiction without any notification. Using this privilege unnecessarily was a sure way to ruin relationships, and without much-needed relationships, you had no ability to solicit confidential informants.

The Oklahoma Bureau of Narcotics seldom utilized the concept of original jurisdiction. As a matter of fact, it was the opposite. The undercover officer had to have confidential sources in communities to infiltrate the drug dealers and drug traffickers. Many of your local officers were in the community day after day patrolling and gathering intelligence information on the most significant drug dealers and their known associates. There was nothing better than a county road deputy who knew everyone, whom they were kin to, and who lived where. The information was invaluable.

The good guys needed to cooperate because the bad guys often did, too. Just like the devil knows no boundaries in an attempt to disrupt the believer's life. He will cross the street, the town, or the state to crush you. He will use anything and anybody to create havoc in the world. The devil knows no boundaries. The good guys have to cooperate across boundaries to defeat him.

Unpredictability is always part of the undercover operation. I've often said that being in an undercover drug deal is like riding a roller coaster except this roller coaster can come off the tracks. Thrills are generous, and every second you're undercover or trying to clear a house on the search warrant, you are surrounded by a high level of unpredictability that could lead to injury or death. You won't find a better example of how fast the roller coaster can come off the tracks than my experience in an undercover transaction with Baker P. Roberson.

We had gathered intelligence information on Roberson who lived in Vernon, Texas. He sold marijuana for profit and had been doing it for many years. We maintained a great working relationship with the Texas Department of Public Safety narcotics units and they were always willing to help. They would give us information, and we would do the same for them when they were looking at suspects in Oklahoma, and we both utilized joint efforts of many defendants. When Texas DPS learned that we had a confidential source who could possibly introduce me undercover to Roberson, they were ecstatic and offered their services to assist us. The Texas DPS positive response was a good sign that Roberson was a good target and needed to go to jail. Narcotics agents always light up when they chase someone for a while and finally get an opportunity to do a case on them.

The confidential source was used to arrange my first meeting with Roberson in January 1990. On a cold, blustery night, the source and I arrived in Vernon, Texas, at Roberson's residence. I had previously seen a photograph of Roberson, but admittedly, it did not prepare me for what I encountered. As Roberson greeted us and invited us into the living quarters of his residence, I immediately noticed how large of a man he was and his long dreadlocks. You have to remember I'm 6 feet and 1 inch tall and Roberson towered over me. He had to be 6 feet 5 inches and 275 pounds, and he looked like a professional athlete.

I did not intimidate easily, but this guy was huge! The situation was shaping up as David and Goliath, at least in stature. He wasn't standing and ridiculing the highest God, but he for sure was violating the law of the land and ruining young people's lives by introducing them to marijuana. I didn't need a sling shot and a smooth stone, all I needed was the lure of easy money and a set of handcuffs. I had to be confident and prepared to take this big guy in a physical confrontation if needed.

I think some of my success undercover was due to the fact that I could come across as a long-haired "good old country boy" with an easy-going nature. I learned a long time ago that a big smile can almost win over anyone. However, I think that I carried a pretty mean looking appearance at times, and later in my undercover career people said on several occasions that I reminded them of a hitman. Roberson and I seemed to hit it off and got along from the beginning. I never felt threatened, but always kept the door in close sight. I did not push the marijuana purchase the first time with him and told him I would come back at a later date. He agreed and even allowed me to return without having the confidential source with me. This was a huge advantage as now I did not have to worry about the safety of the confidential source. Frankly, it was going to be my ability as a law enforcement undercover agent against Roberson's ability to detect me. His skill versus my skills. Could he out maneuver me? I was not going to allow that to happen. By the grace of God, I was going to win this cognitive battle. Plus, I had the protection of the Holy Spirit around me, and that's all I needed.

Several days later, I made arrangements to go back to Roberson's residence in Vernon, Texas, alone to purchase marijuana from him. It was going to be tricky because I did not have the confidential informant with me. You always wonder if they will try to search you for a body wire or if they will try to test you as a law enforcement agent. They may want you to try the drug before purchasing it to eliminate their doubts. As an experienced undercover agent, you always have a story ready on why you do not use drugs. You can be very convincing telling them that you have to have a urinalysis at your job the next day, or you do not use the product that you sell, or you tell him that your wife or girlfriend has threatened you if you come home high. That's always a good one!

The absolute rule as an agent is you never use drugs unless they have a gun to your head, and there is zero chance of survival without it. Thank goodness I was never in that position and could always deflect the use of drugs undercover by a well-thought-out plan and talking my way around the issue. Don't kid yourself; they would test you.

So on this cold January night, I arrived at Roberson's residence with surveillance milling around smartly in the area. I stood on the front porch of Roberson's house, and he immediately ushered me into the living area as he vented his frustration toward the Vernon Police Department about how they were always after him. You could see the hatred in his eyes toward the department, and later Roberson was convinced the Vernon Police Department had sent me to his house to make a case on him, but that actually was not true. They were blamed, but they had nothing to do with the undercover sting operation.

Once in the residence, Roberson was cordial, and we made small talk about the weather. It's amazing how an undercover officer can be talking about the weather, sports, politics, or any other topic, but in reality their mind is 100% on survival and making a case. The mouth is moving and talking, but the mind is on the undercover transaction and how to get the heck out of there in one piece. Even in light of Roberson's physical size, he was polite and had a non-intimidating demeanor. I purchased a handful of marijuana joints. You see, Roberson was adamant that law enforcement did not care about joints, so that is all he sold as a marijuana dealer. I thanked Roberson and told him that I would come back and purchase more from him. He agreed and told me to come back to see him.

As I entered my vehicle and left the area, I thought about what must be going through the dealer's mind at that point. It seems like they get confidence in selling to you because they were not arrested at the point of sale. However, never did we ever only purchase one time. We did multiple transactions to show a pattern of dealing, and frankly, you wanted to guard against making one purchase against an individual and running the risk that they were not a significant dealer. Don't get me wrong; if you deal one time, you are a dealer, but you have to remember at the Oklahoma Bureau of Narcotics our mission is to target significant dealers and secure convictions and lengthy sentences, so they will not be on the street quickly to sell their wares again. Roberson must have been relieved as he saw my taillights drop off into the night.

I again contacted Roberson, and we agreed to meet on January 31, 1990, for me to purchase another quantity of marijuana. This time I had planned on talking to him about driving to Altus, Oklahoma, and delivering me a larger quantity of marijuana. I felt like he could easily deliver 25 pounds of weed. I know that he did not like to do large transactions, but I thought I would bring a "flash roll" to entice him. A flash roll is a large sum of currency that you show the dealer with no intention of giving it to him. Any time you have large amounts of cash, it increases the risk of a rip off. So I had to control the flash and make sure I minimized the ability for Roberson to rob me. I followed the agency protocol and secured $20,000 cash for the flash roll. We all know that the love of money is the root of all evil. We were testing Roberson's love for money.

January 31, 1990, was a cold evening, and that played into my favor because I could hide the $20,000 flash roll in my coat pocket and secure the buy money in another pocket. When I arrived at Roberson's residence, he immediately invited me into the living area and was more cordial than ever. We seemed like long-lost friends. Before we made the transaction, Roberson insisted on going into a large detached garage located behind his residence. I felt very comfortable and made the decision to walk back there with Roberson. After we entered the garage, I was shocked. Several older vehicles were parked in the garage, and many of them seemed to be in very good shape. Roberson was bragging about the vehicles in his garage and told me that his house and all the vehicles had been paid for by selling joints of marijuana. Roberson then told me that he was fifty-one years old and that he'd been selling marijuana for forty years. Oh, what great evidence! This guy was hanging himself with his own words.

I was shocked and somewhat amazed how freely Roberson told me those details, and it was obvious he had a high level of trust in me. We walked back into the house and Roberson sold me joints of marijuana, and I made my way to the front door. I then told Roberson that I wanted a larger quantity and asked if he could bring twenty-five pounds of marijuana to Altus, Oklahoma. Roberson then said he did not like to sell larger quantities, but he had access to it. I was standing in the doorway, opened the front door, and literally stood with one foot outside the door. At that point, I pulled out the envelope, which contained the $20,000 cash. I took the money out and fanned it in front of me and told Roberson that I was serious, had the money, and was ready to make the transaction. I could see the twinkle in his eyes, and I never will forget the words he said to me. Roberson said, "I will be in Altus on February 2nd or I will be dead." I thought that was a pretty powerful statement, and I realized that Roberson would probably show up. The deal was a go.

February 2, 1990, rolled around and we had the plan in place. Roberson had agreed to meet me at the Bunker Hill supermarket in Altus, Oklahoma, and bring twenty-five pounds of marijuana for me to purchase. Surveillance was strategically located around the parking lot and across the street of the meeting location. In addition to several Oklahoma Bureau of Narcotics Agents and local law enforcement, we also had two agents from the Texas Department of Public Safety narcotics unit. I sat in my vehicle and waited for Roberson's arrival and listened over the radio as surveillance was looking out for him. It was the classical hurry up, get into position, then wait.

The surveillance team then advised me that Roberson was spotted and was on his way to my location. He pulled up. I got out and sat in Roberson's car. He was very nervous. This was not the same Baker P. Roberson I had purchased from twice before in Texas. This was a nervous individual who I immediately perceived was out of his comfort zone. I was concerned he could do anything. Harm could be on the horizon. He was talking very fast, even to the point where I could hardly understand him. He asked me if I'd brought the money, and I told him yes and asked him if he had the marijuana. He told me it was not with him, but he could go get it and assured me it was readily available. He then told me to stay put, and he would go obtain the marijuana for the transaction.

As he left from the location, I got on the radio and told the surveillance units that Roberson was acting strange. We had to be on our toes. The surveillance team chose not to continue surveillance on Roberson to the second location as they felt like he was acting too weird, and it may burn the deal if surveillance was detected. The surveillance team was specifically given instructions that after the deal, I would give audio and visual signals, and they were to block Roberson's vehicle preventing his escape from the parking lot. The visual signal was me taking off my baseball cap and waving it. The audio was, "Fred is not going to like this."

The surveillance team then advised that Roberson was on his way back to my location and was traveling through the grocery store parking lot toward my vehicle. Roberson pulled up, and I entered his vehicle but left the car door open. He was even more nervous than ever. He was white knuckling the steering wheel and talking fast. He said, "There it is!" I observed several large baggies of marijuana lying in the floorboard of Roberson's vehicle on the passenger side at my feet. I took a few moments to look at the marijuana, but I could quickly tell it was the real deal. He hastily said, "Give me the money!" I told him it was in the trunk of the car, and I would get it. I gave the audio bust signal and got out of the vehicle, took off my baseball cap and waved it. My back was partially turned to Roberson, so I could draw my .357 revolver from my waistband without being detected. I turned around and shouted to Roberson, "Get your hands up! You are under arrest!"

It's amazing how things go into slow motion at times of great stress. Roberson looked at me, and I looked at him. Time stood still. It seemed like it took an eternity, but I could see him in slow motion turning the steering wheel toward me. This was not good! He had the obvious intent of running me over as I had my gun drawn screaming at Roberson to show me his hands!

The surveillance team was not prepared as we had planned because Roberson's vehicle pulled in the opposite direction when he came back. Both the blockers followed the plan, but they went to the rear of the vehicle instead of the front! It was an honest mistake, but a costly mistake. No one was left to block him from driving the car forward. As Roberson slammed his foot against the accelerator, the car jerked violently toward my location, and I was only a few feet from it! One could argue, at that moment I could have shot Roberson, but I elected not to shoot. The car grazed me as it sped out of the parking lot, but I was not injured. I was a little stunned, but still in the fight.

So the roller coaster started to come off the tracks, and we now had Roberson in a vehicle in a high-speed chase trying to stop him. We were in unmarked cars, but we all had emergency lights and equipment. The Altus Police Department marked units were part of the takedown so they immediately led the chase. I was not intimately familiar with the roads in Altus, so I was having to listen on the radio to catch up to the chase. It was chaotic. The background noise on the radio was making the audio transmissions hard to understand, and the units were all trying to get more help to try to stop him.

A group of agents set up a roadblock to try to stop Roberson in the pursuit. One of the agents was named Gary Stoops. Agent Stoops had his model

870 Remington shotgun cocked and locked as Roberson tried to run him over. Agent Stoops later said that his finger missed clicking the shotgun off of safety or he would have shot Roberson, as there was no doubt in his mind that Roberson was trying to kill him. Obviously, Roberson was desperate, and this usually did not mean good things. A few blocks later, Roberson blew through a second roadblock and again refused to stop. He was in a major flight mentality.

The chase continued on until finally Roberson, traveling at a high rate of speed, lost control of his vehicle and crashed into a parked train. The front end of Roberson's vehicle was smashed and completely lodged under the train.

Two Oklahoma Bureau of Narcotics Agents crashed their units into each other at the same time Roberson crashed. The scene was total mayhem when I arrived seconds after the wrecks. It was a miracle that he wasn't killed on impact, but he wasn't even fazed. I watched as he rolled the driver-side window approximately one-fourth of the way down and attempted to throw the marijuana out of the vehicle. It was actually quite comical. All of his effort of frantically throwing the marijuana out of the window as a concealment tactic was obviously not very successful. The marijuana packages were just dropping right outside his vehicle, a whole three inches from his car.

Officers and agents had guns drawn and surrounded his car. There would be no escape for Baker P. Roberson today. When I got to him, I pulled him out of the vehicle, put him on the ground, and placed him in handcuffs. I asked him, "What in the heck are you doing? You could get somebody killed!" He seemed a little dazed but never said a word. The conversation was more like a dad scolding his son. We placed Roberson in a patrol car, and he was transported to the police department for interrogation. Baker

P. Roberson was finally in custody, hopefully for a long time. His marijuana distribution network was no more.

As we processed the marijuana, a citizen drove up and told us to be careful because he (Roberson) had a gun, and they witnessed him shooting out his car window. We could not find a weapon nor did any of the pursuing officers see Roberson shoot a weapon out the window. However, one of the officers thought that he had observed possibly a police officer shooting out their window at Roberson. So we started asking questions, and it appeared that the two Texas Department of Public Safety narcotics agents were hanging out their window and took shots at Roberson during the pursuit. An OBN supervisor drilled down on it, and they could not determine if shots were actually fired at him, but for sure no one was hit.

Ironically, as soon as the scene was secured, our Texas friends for some reason needed to get back and abruptly left the scene. They had saddled up with us and had been great partners during this investigation, and we could not have done it without those two top-notch law enforcement professionals. Whether or not shots were fired will always be a great mystery.

We went to the local hospital and had the agents from the wreck checked out, and luckily, neither one was hurt seriously. The cars were banged up, and of course we had a string of memos to write. The roller coaster day was over, but I knew we had a long way to go with this case as Roberson would put up a vigorous fight in the courtroom.

As we suspected, Roberson had the monetary resources to hire a formidable defense attorney, and we knew that every action I took would be picked apart and scrutinized to the max. We conducted our preliminary hearing, and the judge found sufficient evidence for Roberson to be bound over on one count of drug trafficking and two counts of running a police roadblock. The hearing was the first hurdle to cross, but the largest mountain was to come, and that was a jury trial. Anything can happen in a jury trial.

The first day of jury selection began, and I was startled as Baker P. Roberson entered the courtroom. He could barely walk, and he seemed to be a shadow of the man I was purchasing marijuana from only a few short months ago. He was even walking with a cane. I didn't know how much of Roberson's appearance was to seek sympathy from the jury or if he had actually aged as much as appeared. I had already learned in my career that the drug dealers were scam artists and would pull anything to sway a juror's vote. They come into court clean shaven with a three-piece suit. Sometimes I have to do a double take just to make sure it's the same person. They indeed can clean up well.

The jury was selected, and now we were ready to present evidence of our case. I was the primary witness. The prosecutor did an excellent job of putting on all the evidence of the undercover transactions and conversations I had with Roberson. They painted a descriptive picture of both the arrest and the chase.

Testifying as an agent is one of the most critical components of our job. We have to be exact and obviously 100% honest. The defense attorney's job is to punch holes in our case and try to make the witnesses unbelievable to the jury. When the defense does not have the facts on their side, they have to create doubt in a juror's mind in any way they can and hope to bring doubt of the defendant's guilt. We must have all twelve jurors agree to the guilty verdict, so often the defense attorney will target who they perceive as a weak juror and try to hang the jury.

As the primary witness, I was on the stand for many hours testifying to my role in the case, and the defense attorney grilled me on everything I had done. The defense was making a huge issue of the fact that we did not follow Roberson's source for the marijuana the day of the buy bust and arrest. I explained on the witness stand that our primary goal was Roberson, and we felt like it might jeopardize the surveillance if we had followed him to the source's location. Like always, the defense was trying to hang their hat on things that did not factually matter in this case. The defense attorney in front of the jury stated that this was the worst police work that he had ever seen. As a law enforcement officer, you just have to sit there and listen to it when you know you did everything right and with integrity.

After several days of testimony, the evidence was completed, and the case rested. It was now in the hands of the jury. This is always a tense time because we never know what is going to happen and what their conclusion will be in the findings. I knew that we did everything right, and I was confident that the jury would return in our favor. So when the bailiff called us all back into the courtroom, I was prepared to listen to the verdict. It was read, and it was an overwhelming decision for the prosecution and the State of Oklahoma!

Roberson was not only found guilty on the distribution of controlled dangerous substances, but he was also found guilty on both counts of running a roadblock. The jury recommended maximum sentence on all counts. The jurors believed us, and we won! This was absolutely a home run, and justice had been served.

I thought about what the defense attorney had said—that this was the worst case of police work he had ever seen, and I jokingly said that if this was halfway decent police work, then Roberson would have received the death penalty. I was very confident we were going to win, but I was relieved when the jury had decided. The Baker P. Roberson era of drug dealing in north Texas and southern Oklahoma was now over.

A short time after the conclusion of the Roberson case, I was transferred to our Ardmore district office and became partners with Agent Gary Stoops who had assisted me on the Roberson arrest. He was nearly run over by Roberson at one of the roadblocks. Gary and I became fast friends and Christian brothers with a mutual interest in gospel music and youth ministry. I spent five years of my career in Ardmore before moving on to another assignment in the state and watched agent Stoops become an unmovable Christian. Stoops was not a perfect man, no one is, but he truly had a passion for Christ.

He was not much of a decorator. He had hung numerous posters, scriptures, and other Jesus memorabilia on his office walls, haphazardly, with not much rhyme or reason. It was not done with great style, but they meant a lot to Gary and clearly quietly voiced his Christian belief.

Many years later as I finished coaching a little league football practice, I was notified that Stoops had passed away from a heart attack. He was in his forties and much too young to leave this world. Although I had not worked side-by-side with Gary in many years, I was in shock. He had several health problems, but his passing was totally unexpected. I traveled immediately to the Ardmore district office to console and support the agents. Then, I drove to the hospital and briefly spoke to Gary's wife. It was a sad day. We went to the Ardmore district office, and I went into Gary's office.

I immediately noticed something that made me smile. After all these years, Gary still had the same posters, memorabilia, and scriptures up on his wall to proclaim his faith in Jesus Christ. They were all basically hung in the same places. He was consistent. He had never given up the faith.

At the time of his memorial service, I was the Director of the agency and had the honor to speak about the life of my friend. I told the many people there I was thrilled from my heart that Gary had kept his faith in Christ, and he had not been moved after all those years. I know Gary was pleased because people reacted to his faithfulness to the Lord Jesus Christ, and that's exactly what Gary would have wanted in the end. I'm looking forward to seeing my friend again one day on the other side.

Matthew 25:21 (NIV) says, *"His master replied, 'Well done, good and faithful servant! You have been faithful with a few things; I will put you in charge of many things. Come and share your master's happiness!'"*

6

THE SPIRITUAL INTERDICTION

Some moments in time influence you forever. Life is made up of day-to-day reoccurring tasks, but on occasion, pure revelation comes to you straight from the throne room of God, dispatched by the Holy Spirit, and you never forget it. Things that happen in the carnal world are called life experiences, but our experiences in the spiritual realm we call "revelations." One event happened that truly changed the compass heading in my life and gave me an understanding and spiritual insight that has guided me since that moment. Through fatigue and a weary body, I received a game changer from the Lord.

In the early 1990's, I was transferred to the Ardmore district office. I was working cases as a Senior Agent. Ardmore is located in south-central Oklahoma, and it is the smallest geographically of the Bureau narcotics districts. We had a wonderful office, and my experience there was very positive. My supervisor, David Taylor, and I developed a deep friendship, and he was one of the best supervisors I ever had as an agent. He always cared deeply for his employees and stood by them even to a fault. He was a former Marine, and his devotion to country and duty were unmatched. He was big and burly, but inside he was a gentle man with a huge heart. We became life-long friends through thick and thin.

We had a secretary named Jonna Fisher who was a devout Christian, piano player, and an incredible gospel singer. She had a voice that should have been on gospel radio stations. The type of voice that would make your spine tingle. Heart-moving music can make a hardened unbeliever become a Christian convert immediately after the first verse is sung. Jonna was the mother hen of the office and was a kind, wonderful woman and an amazing cook. Yes, she was an amazing cook! It's funny how I always remember that important fact.

In addition, Chera Fuller was an incredible investigator in the office and a lot of fun in general. Chera was a journalist by trade and was the most aggressive investigator I ever worked with at the agency. The bad guys did not have a chance when Chera got on their tail. She was a bulldog. When she sunk her teeth in, you were finished. You might as well come and turn yourself in and supply your own handcuffs. She had an unusual talent in that was she was a master of persuading law enforcement agencies to get involved in her cases. No one was immune from being caught in her web. She would have federal, state, and local agencies working on a case and all the officers believed that they were the most important piece of the puzzle. She was a master of persuasion and made everyone feel important, an honorable trait.

Gary Stoops, who ended up being a long-time, strong Christian brother, rounded out the office. Gary was methodical and multi-talented. I was trying to balance the crazy world of narcotics enforcement with a deeper walk with Christ, and the Ardmore district office clan made it easier because of their walks in faith.

The interstate highway system in Oklahoma is well designed and gives you the ability to travel the length of the state from any direction very quickly. Interstate 35 runs north-south from Texas to Kansas, and Interstate 40 runs from the Texas Panhandle to Arkansas. In addition, there is Interstate 44, which runs from southwest Oklahoma to northeast parts of the state into Tulsa and then continues on to Joplin, Missouri. Finally, the Indian Nation Turnpike runs through southeast Oklahoma from Texas northward and connects with Interstate 40. With this sophisticated and vast interstate system, and the fact that Oklahoma is centrally located, our state is considered a main crossroads to large cities in the United States.

Drug traffickers cherish such a highway system that permits them to move quickly at high rates of speed with minimal contact with law enforcement. Many times the individuals that are transporting large quantities of controlled dangerous substances are not the leaders of the cartels or even the intermediates, but are commonly called "mules." Mules are usually low in hierarchy of the cartel. They receive a sum of money to take contraband from one point to the other. The monetary agreement differs at times but usually includes travel expenses and a lump sum of cash for transporting the drugs. The quantity of drugs being transported is usually a reflection on how much the mule is trusted. In other words, the leader is not turning over a hundred pounds of marijuana or twenty kilos of cocaine to someone who is not trusted in the organization. A proven track record of success goes a long way in choosing a mule—very similar to any business enterprise.

One of the specific tasks of the mule is to insulate the primary participants in the drug trafficking organization. Frankly, mules have to be trusted, but sadly, mules are expendable people within the organization, and cartels expect a certain amount of their illicit transports to be interdicted and confiscated by law enforcement. The drug trade is so lucrative that they realize that they do not have to get every load through to market to make an incredible profit.

One of the main things the mules understand is that if they are caught, under no circumstances do they "snitch" and turn over their bosses to law enforcement. If a large sum of drugs or money is lost, they have to go back and explain what happened, and the rumor is that the desert is full of unmarked graves of people who lost large loads.

In the winter of 1991, on a cold Sunday evening, I was attending church service when I received a page to go 10-8 to the Bryan County area. Ten-eight means going into service and to head that direction. An agent does this without question as part of the job. Bryan County was approximately an hour and ten minutes southeast of Ardmore. My blood pumped as I drove down there to assist agents on a drug interdiction stop. As agents, we can go from a normal day at church with family to packing our gear and living a life where danger is right around the next corner.

We were to report to the Bryan County Sheriff's office and receive further instructions. When I arrived at the sheriff's office, I was briefed that an individual was arrested on a traffic stop with several pounds of marijuana and was transporting it to an undisclosed location in Oklahoma. A sheriff deputy's canine unit had alerted on the vehicle and called the Oklahoma Bureau of Narcotics for assistance. The mule who was transporting the marijuana from south Texas was willing to cooperate and assist law enforcement in developing a case against the traffickers who were paying him to transport the marijuana across the state.

When the mule is caught, and the drugs are interdicted before delivery, the next step is a controlled delivery. With the support of the mule, law enforcement agents deliver to the purchaser who is then arrested. It is often difficult to do because of the timing of the original interdiction stop and the fact that mules are not trusted in general.

In this case, the mule was a young man approximately 20 years of age, and his name was Johnny. The case agent attempted to do controlled calls with Johnny, but the purchaser on the other end of the line seemed cautious and was not willing to come to Bryan County and take custody of the marijuana. He apparently didn't trust Johnny. You never know the true personalities of the source nor the mule, so calls can be unsuccessful by the mere fact that the mule called at all. Controlled deliveries are difficult at best.

The night drudged on with multiple calls from Johnny to the purchaser on the other end. One thing about drug investigations is that they are not like the movies. The movies portray a narcotic agent's life as one that is constantly exciting and moving fast when in reality most of the agent's life is spent waiting. I think the old saying says it all, "Drug dealers do not own watches." We were on drug dealer time, and no one was in a hurry. We have undoubtedly exciting moments, but a massive amount of mundane time is spent sitting and waiting, then waiting and sitting. When we are tasked as support or a surveillance team, then we really don't have much to do until the actual deal happens. We try to help the case agent, but he or she is usually doing calls or interviews themselves, and that is really a one-person job. We drink a lot of coffee.

Through all the waiting, I began to notice Johnny and the non-verbal communication he was displaying. He was sitting in a deputy's office distraught with his head held low and seemed to be in a constant mumble to himself. I went into the office and struck up a conversation with him. He immediately struck me as an individual who was beat down and in a heavy cloud of depression. Granted, he had just been caught trafficking marijuana and was in trouble, but I knew this was different than the normal bad guy who just got caught. Maybe it was because he was relatively young or the fact that he seemed mentally slow and reflected a childlike behavior. I could not put my finger immediately on it, but something stirred in my spirit about this guy.

As he sat in the deputy's office, I could hear him speak under his breath that life was not worth going on with because of what he had done. The enemy loves it when we make a mistake, and he seizes those times to beat us down. Where our Lord is passionate, forgiving, and wants us to succeed, the devil has no compassion, never administers forgiveness, and wants us to fail miserably. I then started praying that God would give me the opportunity to speak with him and speak hope into his life. I needed the Lord to give me the words.

Finally, everybody left the office, and Johnny was sitting by himself. I knew I had to seize the moment; it may be my one and only time to talk to him alone. I went in and asked him how he was doing, and he said not well. Then, a strange feeling came over me. I had a strong sense in my heart that the young man would attempt to kill himself in the jail.

The thought overtook me, so I immediately started reassuring Johnny by telling him that he was young and this was just a setback, a life learning experience. I attempted to encourage him by pointing out that he had never been in trouble before; he could survive this and learn from it. I tried to convey to him that he would come out on the other end of this a better person.

Most importantly, I told him that God loved him as much now as He ever did, and while He may be disappointed, He still loved him as a son. God was in the business of redemption, grace, and forgiveness. Nothing he could ever do would separate him from God's love. I tried to speak hope into this young man's life and bring life back into his spirit and heart. He looked at me with great dismay and shock. I think sometimes that criminal defendants think that law enforcement does not care and that we cannot have Christian compassion. We have to do our job, and we have to do it to the best of our abilities, but I never felt like that should stop us from loving the people. I didn't love their deeds nor their further criminal behavior, but I can love them as a person. God told us to love them; judging them was His role.

Some are difficult to love because of how ruthless, brutal, and vicious they are to people in life. However, Johnny was a young man that needed to hear that tomorrow was a new day in his life, and he would get through this. Plainly spoken, Johnny was worth saving. I talked fast, because I knew I only had a moment with Johnny. God's timing is perfect, and I told him everything God had laid on my heart. Immediately following my last words spoken to him, others walked into the room. Our brief encounter was over.

We waited several more hours and attempted to make the controlled delivery, but it never happened. Eventually, Johnny was returned to a jail cell. I never saw Johnny again. I had been through a long day and a longer night. Dawn was about to break and everyone was tired. We called it a night. I loaded up in my Bureau vehicle and start traveling westbound on Highway 70 toward Ardmore to home and a warm bed. I had drunk a lot of coffee, but I was tired enough that it was not going to affect me much. My body was ready for rest.

As I was traveling, fatigued from the evening's labor, I became a little frustrated in a very odd way. I started having a conversation with myself and God. All I could think about was the day was a failure because the controlled drug delivery did not go as planned. I said, "What a waste of time! Why in the world did we go to all of this trouble for nothing; it was for the most part fruitless." As I drove down the road, one of the most compelling spiritual encounters happened, and it was one of those things that changed my life forever.

The Spirit of the Lord spoke to my heart in a very direct way. It was real and weighty. The words the Lord spoke to me have guided me and assisted me in reasoning throughout my life many times. As I was questioning the day, His gripping words moved me as He said, "The world does not revolve around the carnal, but it revolves around the spirit."

It was an amazing moment in my life and a great revelation. The evening was not about whether or not we made a delivery of a controlled dangerous substance with the pursuit of the source. The day was about Johnny's future. I learned later that he survived, and no suicide was attempted in the jail that night. I'm convinced that the Spirit of God intervened, and if not, I'll always believe that Johnny would have attempted suicide.

Clearly the Lord was telling me that there's no action in this world that does not have some type of spiritual connotation. It's not about that moment. We must always look spiritually and see what God is teaching us or what He is doing in that moment.

There is a compelling story in 2 Kings 6:13-17 (KJV) of spiritual eyes being opened when Elisha's servant got confused on who was in the majority.

And he said, Go and spy where he is, that I may send and fetch him. And it was told him, saying, Behold, he is in Dothan. Therefore sent he thither horses, and chariots, and a great host: and they came by night, and compassed the city about. And when the servant of the man of God was risen early, and gone forth, behold, an host compassed the city both with horses and chariots. And his servant said unto him, Alas, my master! How shall we do? And he answered, Fear not: for they that be with us are more than they that be with them. And Elisha prayed, and said, Lord, I pray thee, open his eyes, that he may see. And the Lord opened the eyes of the young man; and he saw: and, behold, the mountain was full of horses and chariots of fire round about Elisha.

This is an incredible scripture. Elisha's servant only looked with his physical sight and viewed a force against them that completely outnumbered them and seemed hopeless. When we look in the carnal many mountains seem unmovable, and it is easy to lose faith. At that moment Elisha prayed, and the eyes of the servant were able to see.

Don't be fooled. The servant could see in the flesh with his eyes. He saw the great mighty army against him, but with Elisha's prayer, the carnal sight shifted to spiritual. The impossible now was possible. Discouragement now was replaced with hope and confidence. At that moment, the servant's eyes saw in the spirit. He saw beyond the natural and saw into the magnificent spiritual world. He saw that more were fighting for their safety and success than were battling against them.

So no matter who you are or what you do in your life—you can be a teacher, doctor, police officer, electrician, bus driver, stay-home parent, accountant, lawyer, electrician, plumber, retail clerk, fireman, banker, or any professional—it doesn't matter because God is no respecter of persons (Acts 10:34 KJV). God loves us equally. Every believer must embrace that the world doesn't revolve around the carnal, but around the spiritual.

The carnal things are subject to change, but the spiritual things are everlasting. Paul wrote in 2 Corinthians 4:18 (KJV) and nailed it, *"While we look not at the things which are seen, but at the things not being seen. For the things being seen are temporary, but the things not being seen are eternal."* This is coming from a guy who had one heck of a spiritual experience on the road to Damascus. He went from a hater of the Christian movement in the flesh to being the author of about two thirds of the New Testament.

So, in every circumstance or crisis, find comfort that God is at work in the situation. We may think the armies are ganged up against us, but praise the Lord, there are more for us than against us!

7

"She will shoot you!"

Several months later, I was enjoying a Sunday night service at church as I prepared to face another week ahead. During the service, I received a page from headquarters that advised me to travel to Bryan County again and assist the drug task force on an undercover drug deal and possibly the execution of a search warrant. Getting a callout was normal, and all agents had to be prepared to go at any moment. We always carried a few days' changes of clothes in our cars because we never knew when we would be hung up overnight or several nights on a deal. As I walked out of the church, I had a funny feeling in my stomach. At this point in my career, I had been on many enforcement actions, but I would still get an adrenaline rush—a rush of excitement and anticipation. For some reason, tonight was different as I pulled away from the church parking lot. I literally felt a tingling feeling going down my spine, and knew I had never felt this feeling before. Something just didn't feel right. I could not shake it, but I discounted it as just being a Sunday night and my evening plans had been altered. I whispered a short prayer and asked that God protect and keep us and that the blood of Jesus cover my life. After I prayed, I started feeling better, and the Holy Spirit gave me a peace. My focus shifted to the task at hand.

When I arrived at the Sheriff's office, I located the briefing room housing approximately ten officers from several law enforcement agencies in the area. My first impression was that we definitely had enough help on this deal. In drug enforcement, we always wanted to have the superior force. In other words, we want more for us than they have for them—more guns pointing at them than pointing at us.

An informant planned to purchase a quantity of methamphetamine from a sixty-eight-year-old individual named Roxie Scott. The deal would take place at her residence south of Durant in a small community called Calera. Scott ran a rough and tumble rural bar. In Oklahoma, we commonly called these establishments a "gun and knife club." As the joke goes, if you did not bring your personal gun or knife, then they would issue you one at the door. You entered at your own risk.

Bar fights were rampant in these rugged joints, and someone was always getting pummeled. As the nights lingered on and the beer and whiskey flowed, the odds increased that someone would come out with a broken jaw. They were also a cesspool of drug use and distribution. Hiding in the lawlessness, distributors would sell their illegal wares.

When the bar owner was also one of the most significant drug dealers in the area, then we knew the place was going to be drug infested. Some bar owners are against drugs, and these places have a chance to stay clean. This was not the case with Scott. She was the main culprit, which compounded the problem. Scott not only was the bar owner and manager, but she also lived in a house attached to the bar.

The informant planned to enter Scott's residence and buy the drugs, then he would simply exit the residence. Immediately after he left with the dope, the raid team would follow in behind him. The team would facilitate the arrest, put much needed handcuffs on Scott, then serve a search warrant for the premises. The warrant included not only the primary residence, but also the attached bar area.

The bust would take some timing, but we had done these types of deals before, and they were very manageable. The informant would be out of harm's way, and we would be able to maneuver into the residence without having to worry about his safety. Besides, the defendant was sixty-eight years of age. What harm could a sixty-eight-year-old female do to this tough group?

I overheard the informant make a statement several times concerning Scott, "She will shoot you!" We hear that type of talk all the time, so we were very accustomed to it. He repeated again, "She will shoot you!" He repeated this several times in a redundant fashion. He said it the last time, "She will shoot you; her ex-husband is in jail for murder; her son is in jail for murder; and her boyfriend has just got out of jail for assault and battery. She is crazy, and she will shoot you!" I was tired of listening to his yapping and was ready to go do the deal.

My assignment was to be the first man through the door, which meant my primary task was to successfully breach the door. The team would follow behind me through the door. Many times the door is breached by kicking it with brute force, and no device, such as a door ram, is used to assist. To old narcotic agents, being able to kick any door open on a search warrant was a weird measurement of strength, especially if a person could pop the door open with one solid kick and not take several attempts. On the other hand, we could look pretty weak if we're taking multiple kicks at a door and we can't get the job done. Even worse, if we can't get the door open and another agent steps up and kicks it open with his or her first kick, not good. All that door kicking is hard on the body. Many a macho drug agent has paid the price of a sore or injured back because of him maintaining his door-kicking pride. Workman's compensation claims have decreased considerably with the invention and acceptance of door rams.

The residence was attached to the bar, but had a separate external door entrance, which we considered the front door. It was the same door the informant would use, and we would file in after he conducted the deal and exited the residence. However, there was one problem. A metal cage built out of steel bars surrounded the front door, possibly a significant barrier if locked. Our timing behind the informant would be critical as we could not allow the target to have enough time to lock the cage.

Once we made entry into the cage, there was an exterior wooden door, and we felt very confident that we could successfully breach it and make entry. It didn't look very difficult. A deputy handed me a metal fireman's tool for a breaching tool, which I graciously accepted. I had never laid eyes on one of these contraptions. I had certainly not ever used one to make entry into a house on a search warrant, but I thought the tool was cool-looking with all its hooks and claws, which admittedly I had no clue as to their proper functionality. As a macho narcotics agent and a quick thinker, I knew I would figure it out when needed. I wouldn't dare ask someone how to use it and expose my ignorance; besides, wasn't I nine feet tall and bullet proof?

We partnered up and loaded into the vehicles with the raid team. The caravan started moving down Highway 69 toward Calera. You have to remember that at this point our adrenaline is pumping 90 miles an hour, and these caravans can get in a hurry. They have a tendency of moving down the road faster and faster. If we are not careful, we will have our raid team strung out miles apart. That is why we have a rally point within a few miles of the target location to regroup and make sure we have not lost anyone. We stopped and counted noses. We determined we were good to go and together made the final mile to the bar.

We let off the informant a short distance from the bar, and we all took covert surveillance positions located in close enough proximity to be able to monitor the body transmitting device we had placed on the informant. The drug transaction went fairly smoothly. Scott allowed him into the residence, and after a short conversation, he scored the methamphetamine.

When the transaction was completed, the informant stuck with the plan. He immediately exited the residence, and walked down the road toward an unmarked undercover car as instructed. We gave the informant time to clear the area, and we proceeded to execute the search warrant.

The team quickly approached the cage. I was in front, on-point, leading the assault and felt very confident. Up to this point, the deal seemed to be going really smoothly. When I made it to the cage, I started to swing the entry tool to knock the door open as we all yelled, "State Police, search warrant!"

The first swing was my first indication that maybe I should have researched the cage and the tool before this grand moment. You see, swinging the tool was nearly impossible due to insufficient space, and I couldn't get a robust swing at the door. Room in the cage was at a premium. My full range of motion was gone, and I was forced to only take short, choppy, and more importantly, ineffective swings at the door.

About that time a shot rang out! Time seemed to stand still, and everything shifted into slow motion. Then it hit me like a ton of bricks. Someone was shooting at us through the door from inside the house! Someone from our team yelled, "They are shooting through the door!!" I immediately dropped the breaching device, moved away from the front door, and frantically escaped the death trap inside the cage. Everyone was scattering.

I made my way quickly to the corner of the house to a much safer position. We didn't know how many people there were or how many weapons. We ask ourselves, are we about to have a major fire fight or will it be a one round fight? The more I thought about the coward shooting through the door the angrier I became. I was fuming, but at this point we could not retaliate and shoot back. In law enforcement, we are trained that we absolutely never shoot unless we have a clear target and threat. Also, we didn't know if innocent bystanders were on the other side who might be hit in a crossfire or a stray bullet. Nothing could be done at this point.

Admittedly, we were not prepared for this moment at all. We all just stood there with no plan, but before we had to think much more about it, the door began to open. It opened remarkably slowly. Then, two hands protruded from the opening in the door. That is all we could see, the hands, and clearly they held no weapon.

The agents placed the individual on the ground, and I immediately recognized her as Roxie Scott, the woman we were after. The remainder of the team hastily went in and secured the remainder of the house and the attached bar. No one else was present in the house. We did find the .38 caliber revolver she shot lying harmlessly on the staircase.

We secured Scott and took her to the county jail. The informant was waiting in an agent's vehicle about a hundred yards from the residence. The windows were heavily tinted, so no one would recognize him. I approached the vehicle and tapped on his window. After several taps, he still didn't respond.

I said, "Hey! Roll down the window." Finally, the informant rolled down the window. He was sitting low in the seat to keep from detection. I stated, "You were right: She will shoot you!" I said nothing else and walked away. The kooky informant who rambled and insisted that she would shoot was spot on. He was right; she shot!

I walked back to the front door of the house to look things over. I stood straight up in front of the door and looked at the bullet hole left as the result of her shooting. At that moment, chills ran up my spine. It so happens that the bullet hole was exactly at my eye level. If I would have been standing up straight, most likely, I would have been shot in the head. As I reflected on the events, I recalled I was leaning over to try to get a good swing at the door due to the tool and the confined space. The trouble I had with the entry tool may have saved my life. God is good!

I was in mild shock by the thought that it all could have ended that day, but God spared me. I really looked at things differently for a while, not as much worry, not as much conflict. Frankly, I was just glad to be alive. It's interesting how such an event can change your perspective on life.

God is in control of everything from the trajectory of a bullet, to the timing of me stooping slightly to get a swing when the bullet passed. He controls it all. I remembered the story of David and Goliath and how God guided the smooth stone from David's slingshot to the forehead of the giant. The precision was not by happenstance or luck. It was the Almighty God who is in control of bullets or any other thing that tries to harm us in our lives.

I told my Pastor about the shooting. He said without hesitation that an angel must have deflected the bullet by his wing. He even used it in a sermon. I am not sure exactly how it happened, but I do know that Psalms 34:7 (NIV) says, "*The angel of the Lord encamps around those who fear him, and he delivers them.*" I will have to ask God when I get to heaven, but all I know is God gave me another day on this earth. He protected me, and it built my faith and courage.

8

CANADIAN COUNTY MARIJUANA FIELD

Oklahoma has physical terrains that are opposites throughout the state. Western Oklahoma is flat, and one can see forever. If we can find a slightly elevated hill, we can utilize it as a nice perch for surveillance because we will be able to see for miles and miles. Trees are scarce, and it's wonderful ground for the wheat farmers, cattle ranches, and most recently the wind farms. By definition, it is "where the wind comes sweeping down the plain" as penned by Oscar Hammerstein's lyrics in the famous song "Oklahoma." Western Oklahoma is the snapshot in most people's minds of how the entire state looks.

The eastern part of Oklahoma is totally different as it displays beautiful mountains. Twelve million acres of Oklahoma are considered forest lands. Also, the Ouachita National Forest in southeast Oklahoma covers 1.8 million acres across central Arkansas and southeastern Oklahoma. These dense lands breed the cultivation of marijuana.

In the 1980's, Oklahoma was one of the largest domestic illicit marijuana cultivation markets in the United States. McCurtain County is the most southeastern county in Oklahoma, and it produced some of the nation's most potent marijuana. It actually was known all over as "McCurtain County Gold." T-shirts and tattoos were designed to glorify the drug that was grown in that region.

Unfortunately, southeast Oklahoma had high unemployment rates and suffered from economic challenges. The people in the area are some of the hardest working, down-to-earth folks; however in the 1980's, competition was stiff for good paying jobs. The geographic location was a benefit to the growers, but demographics were a huge part of it, too. The lure of easy money was very tempting for many. One could grow a thousand plants and yield a pound of product per plant. A pound of good homegrown buds would sell for around $1,000 to $1,500 per pound. You can do the math. A sizable sum of money could be made in the business of cultivation of marijuana, and no other jobs could compare to those profits. The "McCurtain County Gold" was a sure road to "McCurtain County Cash."

The growers were notorious for their violence, and the murder rate was extremely high. Many of the deaths were over dope deals and weed patches. They did not fear the police or sheriff's office, but the growers' worst fear was to be "ripped off," or robbed by another grower. The business was serious and competitive. The uniqueness of this line of work is that it had a life or death component. Many hunters use the area because it is prime deer country as well. Stories circulate of innocent hunters or groups who stumbled upon massive marijuana grows, and not all made it out alive. McCurtain County was an unforgiving world of backwoods bars and cutthroat cultivation tactics. Chicago mob bosses had nothing on these country boys who embraced organized crime, rural Oklahoma style, with chewing tobacco and coveralls.

Although southeastern Oklahoma had an abundance of outlaws, the fact remained that the vast majority of the citizens were hard-working, core-value Christian men and women who opposed drug use and the growing of pot. The light tries hard to overcome the darkness, but at times the pot fields of McCurtain County were really pitch black.

Henry Bellmon recognized the issue with the marijuana cultivators as a serious problem, and he had the power to get something done about the situation. You see, in 1989, Henry Bellmon was the Governor of Oklahoma. This was Governor Bellmon's second round as Governor. The first was from 1963-1967, and he also represented Oklahoma in the United States Senate from 1969-1981.

Governor Bellmon was a well-respected politician and public servant. He understood the outdoors and was actually a farmer by trade. He was comfortable when the public complained to him that they could not even go outdoors in southeast Oklahoma because of the dangerous marijuana culti-vators, and he truly understood their plight.

Governor Bellmon took a sincere fondness to the Bureau of Narcotics and supported us at a high level. I think he felt this way partly because he was a former Marine, and he appreciated the toughness of our agents. One time he was quoted in *The Daily Oklahoman* newspaper that narcotics agents were "a different breed." Of course, the agents secretly loved the compli-ment and wore the comment with a badge of honor. It rightfully set this crazy, courageous group of men and women apart, and honestly, he was not far from the truth.

So in late 1989, the Governor contacted the Oklahoma Bureau of Narcotics Director and told him to form a plan to take the lands in southeast Oklahoma back for the "good" people of Oklahoma. Our marching orders were born. How would we go into the rugged hills and locate, dismantle, and prosecute these violators? At the time, it seemed a daunting task, but one thing you should know about the bureau, we were a creative bunch, and the mission would get accomplished!

The Bureau had always investigated marijuana fields and had done a fairly decent job on the issue, but frankly it was on a small, isolated scale. What the Governor was requesting was an all-out law enforcement assault on the growers and measurable results. As with any law enforcement task, we had to frame the problem, devise a plan, and then formulate training to equip for the task.

The heavily wooded, rugged terrain presented logistical problems of how we could accomplish the directive. We determined that we would have to utilize paramilitary type operations to be successful. The Army National Guards around the nation were forming "Counter Drug" units, which employed a cadre of small reconnaissance helicopters and intelligence analysts.

OBN and the National Guard Counter Drug Unit were a good partnering fit with our similar missions. The partnership benefited us because we had a significant problem to solve, and it helped the guard unit by giving them a very worthy mission in peacetime. So a long-term partnership was birthed. The aircraft would be used with trained marijuana spotters to fly over the rough terrain to locate grows. The intelligence analysts augmented the OBN analysts, provided valuable information, and collected statistical data.

The lands of southeast Oklahoma were not the promise land, but it was definitely beautiful. I was reminded of the biblical story in Numbers 13 when the spies went into the land to scope out what was going on. We didn't have giants, but we sure had a formidable foe with a tremendous foothold who was not going to let go without a battle.

Our relationship with the military department expanded with our introduction to Camp Gruber, which is the Oklahoma National Guard training center. Camp Gruber is 87 square miles located near Braggs, Oklahoma, in the Cookson Hills in the eastern part of the state.

In 1989, Camp Gruber housed an air assault course, a demanding course of instruction after which the graduate is qualified to rappel from a helicopter. This unique set of skills was exactly what was needed to tackle the marijuana fields and rugged terrain of southeast Oklahoma.

This skill would save countless man hours of literally walking in brush looking for a field. The spotter aircraft would spot the grow, then a team by aircraft could safely come from above and be dropped in the field by rope, or the aircraft could find a safe place to land near the field where the agents could deploy for eradication. It would definitely save a lot of time, sweat, and energy. You have to remember that Oklahoma summer days normally have a daytime high in the mid to upper 90's, and many times the temperature exceeds the century mark! So a helicopter ride and a short bound down the rappel rope was a magnificent improvement. I think you get the picture.

The class also taught skills that we could carry over to our everyday law enforcement activities. These skills included small unit tactics, raid planning, writing operation orders, navigation techniques, booby trap recognition, and first-responder training. All were actions that could be used every day in this line of work.

In May of 1989, our first agents were trained at Camp Gruber at the military air assault course. The week started off with the obstacle course. It's a grueling challenge that really wants to measure two things, our upper body strength and our fear of heights. Both of these components are critical when you get to the rappelling stage of instruction.

I didn't have any problems with the obstacles and had the strength to complete them at a high level. However, the height issue was another story! I had never thought about being afraid of heights, and here I was, only a few feet off the ground, and literally scared to death. I knew I had to overcome this fear or I would never graduate. The fear of heights snuck up on me. It blindsided me. This was different than a plane or helicopter ride which never bothered me. I had walked around my entire life and never realized I was not made to leave the ground. Now was a nice time to discover this!

Part of me thought if God had wanted humans to fly then He would have given us wings and feathers. Isaiah 40:31 (NIV) says *"They will soar on wings like eagles; they will run and not grow weary, they will walk and not be faint."* I still questioned if this scurrying down a rope was for me. I admit it is amazing what peer pressure and the concept of team will make you do.

I know several agents were scared like I was, but nobody would show or verbalize it. I decided that God promised He would never leave me nor forsake me, and this included hanging out of a helicopter on a rope. Eventually I started getting more comfortable and graduated the class. Ironically, I eventually went on to the advanced Rappel Master Course, which allows you to be in charge of all the rappellers on the aircraft, and the lives and safety of the rappellers are in your hands. I overcame my fear of heights even to the point of being able to hang out of a helicopter at 1,000 feet only attached by a rope. You can't tell me God is not still in the miracle business!

The school had a huge draw because we learned how to rappel out of a helicopter and the many other valuable components to the program, but arguably the most important aspect was that it put us in the woods for many days with a group of officers and agents resulting in the development of lifelong friendships. That was of great value.

In the early 1990's, we started a full-fledged attack on the marijuana cultivators in southeast Oklahoma utilizing our new aircraft and paramilitary skills. It captivated the attention of Oklahomans, and many articles were written across the state about the rugged and dangerous job the agency was doing in the treacherous hills near the Arkansas state line.

Governor Bellmon got in on the action too. He loved the outdoors, and he really liked the pioneering and tough narcs with their 50-pound packs on their backs busting brush. He flew to Idabel, Oklahoma one day to observe the operations. Some of the locals did not care much for us conducting business in their neck of the woods. As the Governor's plane was orbiting around a few large marijuana patches, one of the local good ole boys decided to try to shoot it down. They were unsuccessful, and the Governor landed safely on his way to the command post.

As you recall, Governor Bellmon was the first Republican elected Governor for the State of Oklahoma and took office in 1963. Then he was the elected to the U.S. Senate in 1969 and re-elected to the office of Governor in 1987. Bellmon was one of the first Republican politicians in Oklahoma. He also had a wonderful, quick sense of humor. When he arrived at the command post with his entourage, he was met by one of the Bureau's K-9 units who immediately barked and attempted to bite the Governor. With his quick wit he said, "He must be a Democrat!" We are still belly laughing over that one!

Even though the majority of the marijuana located and seized was in the southeast quadrant of the state, a lot of weed was still being grown all around the state. It just took more work to find it.

From the air, the trees even looked more scattered and rare, but on the ground they actually could be rather dense. We would select a geographic area and conduct what we referred to as a mission. We would send reconnaissance helicopters a week in advance and they would start gridding an area. The pilots flew the aircraft, and we would train a spotter to be the front seat observer to spot the grows.

The spotters would also be looking for other aircraft, high line wires, and any other hazards. They still had to have the ability to spot marijuana without having motion sickness from the constant spinning. Some people have that talent, and some people don't. I know spotters who can spot one small plant while on the move at an altitude of 1,000 feet. I have spotted patches in my career, but admittedly I was never very good at it. As you might have guessed, I was preoccupied with motion sickness. Refer to Chapter One.

The two things marijuana needs to grow are sun and water. With those two ingredients, the weed can flourish and become a very hearty plant that seems to grow when nothing else is growing. In drought and in monsoons, it will grow. Rumor has it that an agent spotted some growing in an inch of snow. Can't verify that one, but I do know it seems like it has an incredible will to live.

In the summer of 1998, we were conducting one of our eradication missions and this particular operation was headquartered out of Westheimer Air Field located in Norman. Norman is just south of Oklahoma City and part of the metro area. We were covering all counties around the metro and communities within an approximately 100-mile radius.

The spotters had located several nice plots, and they wanted the team leaders to go airborne and view the patches from the air, which gave them a good look at the patch for planning egress and regress routes. Aerial recon is overall good intelligence information and allows us to get our bearings to lead the mission.

I loaded into the aircraft with another team leader, Walter Harkens, and we pulled pitch. We first flew north of the Oklahoma City metro to Payne County near Stillwater and the Cimarron River. Reconnaissance had located a patch in which cultivators were utilizing the river for their water source and for a covert way in and out of the patch via the water. The area had a lot of sand dunes, which translated to us as some soft ground to lie on for an overnight surveillance.

We flew to the outskirts of the Oklahoma City metro and flew over the second patch. We saw typical western Oklahoma terrain. Plowed fields stretched as far as the eyes could see, and a patch of dense trees was located sporadically around each mile section. Over the headset the pilot verbally directed me to view a set of trees that appeared a quarter of a mile ahead. We were at approximately 1,500 feet, and I was concerned that I would not be able to recognize the plot at this height.

As he positioned us over the target, the marijuana stood out like a beacon in the night. Several hundred well-manicured, healthy plants were visible that had been well taken care of in spite of the hot weather. Another thing that caught my eye was the path to and from the patch seemed extremely worn. The path was worn down to dirt. Someone had spent a lot of time and effort for this crop.

Harkens outranked me, so he had first selection on which patch he wanted his team surveilling. My guess was right, and he chose the Cimarron River patch. That left my team with the Canadian County patch, but I was still very pleased. I liked what I saw from the air.

We arrived back at the Command Center, and I briefed my team on the findings and presented the game plan. We would gather our gear for an overnight stay and set up an ambush in the field in hopes the cultivators would come water or tend to their crops in some way. I had no doubt in my mind by how much the paths were worn that someone or a group of someones had put great effort into this field daily.

Our mission would only be for one night because we had VIPs and the press coming the next day to view the grow. So we planned to go in and set up throughout the night and maintain security at the location before and while the dignitaries were on site. Part of the security sweep would be the location and disbarment of any booby traps, which was always a concern.

Another thing we learned in our training at Camp Gruber was how to survive in the woods for long periods of time. We would train on packing our gear, food, water, rain gear, bullets, etc. for overnight or multiple days and nights of surveillance. It was hot, draining work, but we got good at it. We set up "L" ambushes in the field and waited for the cultivators so we could actually observe and gather evidence as they worked their crop.

The record for me in my career was four days and three nights, and it rained on us during that entire mission. We learned the meaning of perseverance and patience. I always became closer to the Lord when I was in the woods with the quiet of nature all around me. I had time to reflect and gain a renewed thankfulness for all that was around me, not to mention it allowed for some good reading time. Being silent was essential in our success. We couldn't pass time by fellowship and visiting.

I had one song that I sang under my breath every time we were covertly advancing to a patch. It was an old gospel song named, "God Walks The Dark Hills." The tune was perfect because it spoke to how He guides our footsteps. Many times I had a heavy ruck sack on my back with machine gun in hand, stumbling in ill light to make my way through brush and briars to meet our objective. I have learned that God truly guides our footsteps, whether in the woods tracking marijuana violators or in every concrete jungle in the world. God does not change, and He will guide your footsteps.

My team of six heavily armed agents descended upon the drop-off spot for us to exit the vehicles. We had drivers, so we could move quickly, and the vehicles could leave the area with no sign of us. Getting everyone out quietly and off the roadway safely was critical and tricky. The deployment was a success and before we knew it, like clockwork, the team was all across the fence hunkered down in some bushes as we quietly listened for sounds or movement. We heard nothing but silence.

We started slowly making our way in single file moving cautiously, but deliberately. The path was well worn, and I decided that I would not take the team on it because we would leave footprints and be compromised if someone came in behind us. After about 100 meters in the rough, we came across some thick briars and the movement slowed considerably. I decided to move the team to the trail, at least until we got around the thickets.

We made our way to the trail at a deliberate pace. Suddenly, I caught movement ahead out of the corner of my eye. I immediately raised my hand in the air with a closed fist, which is the small unit communication to freeze and not move. The team did exactly as they were trained. We waited for what seemed like an eternity.

Finally, the movement started to take shape as it approached us from the distance. We could see an individual walking toward our team. I immediately pointed to my eyes, then held up one finger. This indicated to the team that I saw one individual. We lowered ourselves slowly into crouching positions.

Then in the distance, I could see a second individual. He was following the first one walking toward us. I immediately indicated to the team that a second person had been spotted. I was concerned at that point whether more were coming. We were not out-numbered, but that is the way I wanted to keep it.

As the two individuals were briskly walking toward us, my mind started planning how we could set up a hasty ambush on them for a confrontation. A chill then ran down my spine as I noticed that the individuals' trajectory was now turning directly toward us. Yes, I knew for certain now, they were on the same trail we were on and heading straight toward us. There would be no chance for an ambush and no place to take cover in case of a gun fight.

I started to make out clearly that both had their shirts off, the first individual was pushing a wheel barrel, and the second one appeared to be carrying something. They did not appear to be armed with any weapons, at least what I could see. I realized the second individual was carrying a white five-gallon plastic bucket. This type of bucket was very common among marijuana cultivators to carry water to their plants when they did not have a hose or a close water source. I knew for sure these men were involved in the grow, but wondered how many more were there in the woods or the field? Was this just the tip of the iceberg? The path was well worn, which concerned me of the possibility of more cultivators, but I had no time to worry about the what-ifs. We had two for sure, and they were headed right toward us!

I whispered a prayer under my breath, "Father protect us and help us survive this confrontation." My prayer was short, but if you think about it, most prayers were short in the Bible. I think the world wants us to believe that we can only call on the name of our Lord in prayer when we have time to pray some lengthy, elaborate prayer. God hears the short prayers too. Don't get me wrong, I believe in the prayer closet and spending time with God, but God does His best work sometimes on short notice and acts on simplicity. Short notice was being defined before our eyes.

We patiently waited. They were getting close, and we were hunkered down on the trail out of sight. Thank goodness we had a slight bend in the trail right where we had stopped. They were now only approximately ten meters away, now eight, now six meters. The hair on the back of my neck was now rising. We had no time to wait. We had to move now!

I placed the rifle on my shoulder and jumped to my feet and yelled, "State Police! Don't move!" The cultivators stopped dead in their tracks. Their eyes were huge, and we startled them to say the least.

The remainder of the team behind me followed suit and sprang to their feet with weapons pointing at the individuals. Then the oddest thing happened, for a moment, time stood still. They did not move; we did not move. I was staring at them, and they were staring back just as hard. We could literally hear each other breathe as our hearts raced. The tension was thick. We froze with rifles, and they froze with a white bucket and a wheel barrel.

People in times of crisis will choose between "fight or flight" in response to stress. They either try to fight their way out of the situation, or they run away to perceived safety. I could see the look in the eyes of the man in the rear. I could tell he was about to make a decision to remedy his situation.

Then it happened. He dropped the bucket in a split second, and he turned around and started running for his life. The race was on. I immediately grabbed the front individual and escorted him onto the ground. He decided not to choose fight or flight, he chose just to stand there in shock. I instructed an agent to stay with him. The agent who secured him was 6 feet and 1 inch tall and weighed about 275 pounds. I was certain the bad guy was not going anywhere.

The race was on for the fleeing subject. He had a distinct advantage because we had to handle his partner, which allowed him a head start, but more importantly, he knew the terrain. Marijuana fields might be booby trapped. He would have knowledge of the traps (if any) and could sprint through the patch easily avoiding any devices.

We, on the other hand, had no idea if the field was trapped and the location of any harmful instruments. We had to be cautious as we navigated through the field yet still give chase. Also, it was apparent he did not currently possess a firearm, but he may have had one stashed and could retrieve it for a gun battle.

I was cautiously running, but knew I needed to get air support as soon as possible. I grabbed my handheld radio and started calling for one of our aircraft. We had an extensive operation going with several aircraft in the air. Surely someone would hear me and come with the much needed air platform to find this clown. The perpetrator can outrun a man on foot busting brush, but to outrun a helicopter is much more difficult. Plus the sun was rapidly setting in the west, and darkness was looming to become our enemy. If we did not locate him soon, the night would almost guarantee his escape. The situation was intense, and the remainder of the team was working their way through the maze of trails in the patch. Then I heard one of the task force officers screaming, "Let me see your hands!" I ran to the aid of the officer, and as I approached, I noticed an individual hidden behind a small tree. The scene was a little comical: The tree was too small, and you could see his legs and boots protruding from behind the tree—not much concealment there.

The bad guy was caught and secured in handcuffs. He evidently had the willpower to run but lacked the physical endurance in the sultry Oklahoma heat to last long in his flight. We were all relieved that the pursuit was over, but we had little time to relax. Suddenly, all we could hear was a vehicle honking its horn in the distance. We were in secluded Oklahoma farm country. As we say, "Not many people in these parts." So why was a car continually driving up and down the mile section line honking its horn?

You don't need rocket science or twenty-five years of investigative experience to figure this one out. Not one vehicle was on the road when we entered the area. Therefore, the cultivators had to have someone drop them off, and now that someone was driving up and down the road like a "Nervous Nellie."

We had deployed a team member on security to the road. He confirmed the presence of the vehicle. I decided to take the team back to the road and set up an ambush for the third conspirator if he decided to make his way into the patch.

Finally, the individual parked his vehicle and made his way toward the patch to check on his partners in crime. He was moving quickly down the same well-worn path where only a short time before we had our standoff.

He eventually made his way to our ambush, and we drew down on him. He was completely taken by surprise and gave up without a fight. He was the son of one of the previous arrestees. We thought it was sweet of them to keep it all in the family.

We called for ground agents to come assist in transporting the three arrestees to jail and book them for cultivation of marijuana. After they were transported, the team went back to the patch and set up for the night. Even though I was confident that we had the primary defendants in custody, you never knew if more conspirators would arrive or if the competition would learn of the arrest and come try to abscond the crop.

The best case scenario is to cut the weed and get the heck out of there, but we had a "Very Important Person" day set for the following day during which several heavily guarded dignitaries would be escorted into the patch to observe the Bureau's marijuana eradication program. The agents in the trenches quietly termed them "dog and pony shows." Most "working stiff" agents were not fans of VIP days, but they had their value when educating politicians and policy makers on our work.

We endured a hot and humid night with bugs, flies, and our regular attendees, the Oklahoma mosquitoes. Pesky little oversized flies that bite and suck our blood out of us—very irritating to say the least. To add insult to injury, we learned that the arrestees were allowed to post bond and did not even spend one night in jail.

That night our team consisted of a task force of officers from various departments. The Bureau of Narcotics, the Norman Police Department, and the Oklahoma Highway Patrol to name a few. Sadly, one of the task force members who lay in the summer heat that year would later be shot and killed in the line of duty while executing a search warrant in 1999. He left behind a wife and two children.

It shows the uncertainty of life. James 4:14 (NIV) says, *"Why, you do not even know what will happen tomorrow. What is your life? You are a mist that appears for a little while and then vanishes."* Here today and gone tomorrow. You cannot put your trust in this world because it's not going to last. Our hope and trust has to be in the One who conquered death, hell, and the grave. Praise the Lord!

9

METH, MONEY, AND GUNS

I n many years of working undercover narcotics, we conducted investigations on all types of targets and defendants. Many in the drug world
were not violent and sadly were addicted-based traffickers who just wanted to survive in a dangerous world and ensure their habits were satisfied.
"Addicted-based violator" was one who never made any money at the drug
trade because most of his profits were gobbled up by the needle in his arm
or the pipe he was toking on.

In contrast, the "economic-based violator" had one thing in mind and
that was to make profit off the backs of the addict. They could be users too,
but often they were business people who did not get entangled in the wares
they were peddling.

No drug is more insidious than methamphetamine. I would rather go undercover against any drug trafficker other than someone selling methamphetamine. With cocaine, heroin, marijuana, pills, etc., the dealers were easier
to deal with and more predictable than someone on meth. In simple terms,

people on meth are absolutely crazy! Meth is extremely addictive because it increases the dopamine in the brain. It affects the reward and pleasure center of the brain by a rapid release of dopamine, which produces a euphoric experience. Users often attempt to recapture the original "high" they experienced, thus this vicious cycle of using more of the drug to re-capture the original high. They take more of the drug in a downward spiral into darkness.

A sheriff friend of mine said it best, "Methamphetamine is the devil's candy. It will take you where you never want to go and keep you there longer than you ever wanted to stay." It's straight from the depths of hell.

The lure of easy money in the drug trade is very appealing to many. They can have a return on their investment of a hundred-fold by selling drugs, and it can be even more lucrative if they manufacture it themselves. The manufacturing of methamphetamine has a profitable return on your investment.

Methamphetamine was first developed in Japan in 1919 and was used as a stimulant. The Kamikaze pilots used it before their suicide missions. Throughout the 1900's, it was prescribed as a diet aid in the United States. In 1970, it became illegal, and motorcycle gangs started producing and distributing the drug. Thus, one of the first slang terms for methamphetamine was "crank" because it was hidden in the crank shafts of the motorcycle gangs. Meth was a cheaper substitute for drug users who could not afford the higher priced cocaine.

The primary meth source now is the Mexican cartels who smuggle the drug across the border into the United States. Domestic manufacturing produces smaller quantities and rarely produces pounds of the product. They are considered "mom and pop" laboratories because of their lack of sophistication. Labs exploding and catching surroundings on fire is a huge concern.

The lure of fast money in the drug business is never more evident than with meth. Producers can purchase the chemicals in a local retail store for a nominal cost, make the meth, and sell the finished product with a huge profit. Nothing can give such a high return on investment (ROI) than methamphetamine production.

The lure of money in this world is interesting. 1 Timothy 6:10 (KJV) says, *"For the love of money is the root of all evil: which while some coveted after, they have erred from the faith, and pierced themselves through with many sorrows."* Greed causes people to do crazy things.

Jesus was interested in how people conducted themselves with their money and watched closely how they behaved with their funds. Mark 12:41-44 (NIV) says, *"Jesus sat down opposite the place where the offerings were put and watched the crowd putting their money into the temple treasury. Many rich people threw in large amounts. But a poor widow came and put in two very small copper coins, worth only a few cents. Calling his disciples to him, Jesus said, 'Truly I tell you, this poor widow has put more into the treasury than all the others. They all gave out of their wealth; but she, out of her poverty, put in everything—all she had to live on.'"*

Where your heart is, your money will be also. The devil is a liar, and he has a formidable combination attack. He uses the lure of money along with the addict's own desire, then he throws in the normal dose of sexual lust through pornography, and the result is a three-punch combination.

The meth trade was unique in that it had cell groups of individuals in a given community who normally were run by an alpha male of the group. The dominant male in the group often had a reputation for being tough and most likely had spent time in prison.

The main control tool the leader had over the group was the fact that he controlled the meth in the community, and they needed him for their addiction. Eventually, they relied on him for much more than just the dope. They looked to him for the basic needs of life: food, shelter, transportation, and protection. Often he would also have several female groupies who would be a part of his sexual harem. Meth was powerful and people did unthinkable deeds for their fix.

The alpha male would use fear and intimidation as his leverage to get what he wanted. He would have enforcers around him that were addicts, and they would beat people and carry out his dirty work. They would get reputations in local communities and scare and intimidate the good citizens. People would walk on the other side of the sidewalk if they saw him coming, for good reason, because meth people are so unpredictable and unstable. Many times, even local law enforcement was intimidated.

People ask why law enforcement uses an overwhelming show of force with an abundance of manpower when conducting a search warrant. Obviously, we want more for us than against us. We want to put the odds in our favor.

Also, we never know when we may run across a "real" bad guy. Everyone in the drug world will talk a good game about being mean, but few are actually violent. The problem is, we never know for sure when someone will actually fight it out with us. I do believe that past history of violence is a good indicator that they possibly will want a confrontation, but we just never are sure.

That is why we have to prepare for the worst case scenario. With each enforcement activity, we must include in our planning a comprehensive operations order that will detail the defendant's criminal history and significant intelligence known. We attempt to mitigate risk. I do believe that the vast majority of individuals involved in the illicit drug world are not looking for a fight with law enforcement.

One exception was Kent Mazzi, a resident of Lincoln County, located between Tulsa and Oklahoma City. He had a reputation as a major methamphetamine manufacturer and trafficker, but even worse, he was by definition a home town terrorist and had a violent reputation.

We had gathered intelligence on Mazzi for several years. We knew where he lived and confidential sources had given us reliable information on his drug ring, which he ruled with an iron fist. He was the ultimate alpha male. He controlled everything around him: money, drugs, guns, women, and he had terror running through his veins. The stronghold the devil can have on people is fascinating and terrifying.

Our intelligence sources informed us that Mazzi was producing large quantities of methamphetamine around his residence. We started hearing that he was looking for a travel trailer to purchase and bury for an undercover meth laboratory.

We would hear rumors of people talking of such elaborate schemes to conceal their labs, but seldom do we come across someone who would go to that much trouble. Remember, Mazzi was an old outlaw, and he would do anything to conceal his lucrative meth manufacturing.

His primary residence was located in Sparks, Oklahoma, but we learned that he had access to a plot of land a few miles from his primary residence in rural Lincoln County. The details of his plans to bury the mobile trailer for an underground methamphetamine laboratory were becoming more real and a possibility.

We conducted aerial surveillance and photographed the property looking for clues. Finally, we found concerning evidence from the air, a bulldozer, and a fresh mound of dirt. The area was large enough that it could easily house an underground trailer, but we needed more evidence.

Then we received information from a confidential source that put our probable cause over the top. We finally had enough to run a search warrant on Mazzi's residence and the rural property for the buried lab.

The morning started like so many in my years at the bureau. It was a hot and humid July morning that started with an early morning alarm, hot coffee, and an adrenaline rush. I always drove too fast to get to the briefing area on these mornings. I am not entirely sure why, but I know we speed to get to the briefing spot just to stand around and wait for two hours.

As we wait for all the teams to arrive, we stand around and tell war stories and visit with other agents we might not have seen in a while. It is usually very upbeat as the atmosphere is very casual and rings with sounds of laughter among friends.

I often think of it as a team before a sports event when the coach insists you "be loose." However, it never failed that when the briefing started and the final instructions were given, the atmosphere changed to one of detail and focus. The stakes here were not a win or a loss on a team record, but the stakes were life or death. It was time for the dedicated men and women to do their job, to put their lives on the line.

This briefing was no different than any of our briefings as it ended with a prayer of protection. As we prayed, one could hear a pin drop. A powerful thing to behold is the reverence of tough men and women who stop for a moment and confess their reliance and seek protection from Jehovah God. I was always in awe. The Bible declared in 2 Thessalonians 3:3 (NIV) *"But the Lord is faithful, and he will strengthen you and protect you from the evil one."*

I firmly believe that the struggle was good vs. evil: the Lord and righteousness vs. satan and sin. Today, we would be instruments of the Lord. Isaiah 41:10 (NIV) gives us great courage by saying, *"So do not fear, for I am with you; do not be dismayed, for I am your God. I will strengthen you, and help you; I will uphold you with my righteous right hand."*

We departed the offsite briefing area and had several miles to travel to conduct the enforcement raids. We had two locations we were going to hit simultaneously. One was Mazzi's primary residence in Sparks, Oklahoma, and the other was the rural location a few miles away, which (based on our reconnaissance) we believed was the location of the buried methamphetamine laboratory.

Dawn was just breaking as the teams made their way to the locations. I held the rank of Agent-In-Charge at the time and could choose which location I wanted. I decided to go with the team to the underground lab location, and we traveled there without a hitch, exited our vehicles, and approached the suspected site. The entry team made their way down into the bunker as the remainder of the team covered the perimeter and watched for other bad guys. Within a minute, they reappeared and gave the thumbs up. This signaled to us that the team was safe, and they had found the methamphetamine lab just as our surveillance and intelligence had indicated. We were right.

My phone rang, and it was a senior agent from the other location. I could hear the anxiety in his voice, and I immediately sensed something was wrong. He was talking fast as he said, "You need to come quick. Mazzi barricaded himself in a bathroom and pulled a gun on us, and Tommy shot him!"

I quickly told him I was on my way. I ordered a small security team to keep the laboratory location secure, I loaded up several of the team members, and we headed to the other location. I was driving a pickup, and we had an agent in the cab and some in the back hanging on for dear life as I made haste to get to the scene.

Even though we obviously drove unmarked undercover vehicles, we had undercover red lights and emergency equipment. They were needed that day. We raced approximately three miles down the country road with agents in the back being tossed around like rag dolls. The adrenaline was in overdrive as my mind was racing thinking of what we would find when we arrived.

After only minutes we arrived at the location, but that brief period of time seemed like an eternity. We pulled up in front of the house, and many of the officers and members of the raid team were in the front yard. I approached the team who naturally looked like they were in shock.

I was escorted into the house and taken to the bedroom in the back of the residence. I walked in the bedroom and immediately noticed two television screens. One was showing pornography and the other was displaying images from a security camera that was in the front of the house. He could see clearly if anyone was approaching the house. There was no doubt from the camera view that he had warning the raid team was hitting his house.

We then entered the bathroom, and I witnessed the poster for methamphetamine and its tragic consequences. Every teenager who wanted to experiment with drugs needed to see this horrible picture. It was by definition the horrendous results of sin.

Mazzi was lying naked in the bathroom floor, his entire body leaning against the toilet. He had a sawed-off shotgun in one hand and a bag of methamphetamine in the other. The hand that held the meth was halfway in the toilet as if he was trying to flush the contraband. He lay there lifeless; he was dead.

Imagine drawing your last breath in that position, leaving this world in that scene. Imagine, leaving earth and waking up in front of Jehovah God and having to account for your actions. My role is not to judge Mazzi and his last day on earth, but it grieves my spirit to see the devil at work at such a high level.

That was the final moment of his life. I wondered what was the first moment in his life that took him to such demise and destruction. My mind drifted back to King David. During the springtime, King David should have been out fighting and leading the Israelites in battle against the Ammonites. Instead, he stayed back and decided one evening to take a stroll on the roof of his palace. That is when it happened. He saw a beautiful woman bathing. Her name was Bathsheba. The King sent messengers to get her even though he knew she was married. She came to him, and they slept together. After that moment in David's life, it was never the same. She became pregnant, and the King was the main conspirator in the death of her husband Uriah. Evil followed David's house: rape, murder, and rebellion. It all started with one moment of time with a glance from a rooftop.

How did Mazzi's start? What rooftop was he on when it happened? Should he have been somewhere else when they offered him his first joint of marijuana as a young man? Did he tell his parents that he was at Jimmy's house when in fact he was at Donnie's house where he knew he shouldn't be at the time. When they rigged the first syringe of amphetamine, was there laughter in the room or a devilish jubilee? I can almost guarantee at that moment he did not play his life out and see the final scene. Just as David didn't on the rooftop.

The agents briefed me on what happened. The team had made entry and immediately engaged a female who later was identified as Mazzi's girlfriend. An agent put her on the ground in the living room at gunpoint. As they made their way to the rear of the house they witnessed Mazzi rolling out of the bed with a weapon in his hand. Mazzi headed toward the bathroom and barricaded himself behind the door.

The team was desperately trying to break down the door. The next moment flashed before their eyes and time stood still. Agent Tommy Walker, a young agent who had not been with OBN very long, kicked the door. What happened next was strange. You see, we do this every day, and when most doors are kicked in, they break lose at the hinges or rip away from the door frame, but not this door. It responded to the kick in a way I had never seen before, nor have I seen since. The door split perfectly in half. This is unheard of, but yet it happened. Because of how the door split, the top half swung open and fell off of its hinges.

Mazzi was crouched in a low kneeling position with the shotgun in his hands, a perfect tactical position. Then when the door split, it somehow came slamming down on his leg. At that critical moment, he winced in pain, and it delayed him as he raised the shotgun toward the agents. It gave the agent a micro second to respond first. Agent Walker shot two rounds in rapid succession. The first round ran down the barrel of Mazzi's weapon and entered his arm. The second round struck Mazzi in the heart. It was a fatal shot, ended the gun battle, and saved several other lives.

Although Mazzi had the superior position and the superior weapon in the close-quarters gun fight, he was unable to get a shot off. No agents were shot or injured. The odds were against us, but our God protected us yet again. Agent Walker, the young man who shot Mazzi that day, progressed through his career and became a devout Christian and an unashamed witness for Jesus. He became a bright light to the young agents at the bureau. He was protected that day by the almighty hand of God. It reminded me again that He loved us, even before we loved Him.

The atmosphere was interesting and telling of the great compassion and humanity of the law enforcement personnel on scene. Even though everyone was relieved to survive the incident, they all realized the significance that someone had lost his life that day. The loss of any human life is difficult. No one arose early that morning and expected to have such a violent encounter. Granted, Mazzi brought it on himself, but there's no doubt everyone there wished he would have just given up and gone to jail. Instead, he elected to be that one in a thousand bad guy who will choose to shoot it out with us.

The scene turned from a drug search warrant to a death. We contacted our sister agency, the Oklahoma State Bureau of Investigation, to come and investigate to ensure the independence of the inquiry. We locked the residence down as the agents had to get another search warrant for the body.

The after effects lingered for several months. I learned something valuable that day that I carried with me my entire career. Traumatic incidents affect people in different ways, and you can't be fooled into believing that a seasoned agent or officer is going to be less affected by them than a rookie. Many times seasoned agents have many incidents built up inside themselves and must later reveal the psychological effects of not dealing with the stress and the impact it has on their lives. A veteran officer works for 20 years; I can guarantee that he or she has captured a lot of images and incidents in his or her memory. If they do not deal with them as they come along, then the pressure is sometimes so overwhelming. I believe that is one of the major causes of suicide among veteran law enforcement officers. They just never seem to have enough opportunities to get the trauma out of their systems. Then the dam of life breaks.

On the other end of the spectrum, you have the young agent who has not yet had many experiences, tragedies, or high stress moments on the job. We had several out there during this time, and I was watching them closely. I told myself that this will make or break these agents. All the agents were required by mandate to see a counselor. Most cops think it's a waste of time, but I strongly disagree. We have to keep our law enforcement personnel in a healthy place, whether mentally, physically or psychologically. We must protect the ones who are sworn to protect us.

I know personally I could not imagine facing troubling times without having the Holy Spirit in me as the greatest psychological counselor of all time. He was always my ready help in time of need—always on time, always bringing peace to my soul.

10

THE ULTIMATE SACRIFICE

The evening of November 11, 2005, started like many Friday nights in Oklahoma: high school football, and not only football, but the playoffs in Moore! The whole town is drawn in to see the local heroes as they battle other teams from around the state to seek after a state championship and a gold ball. The Westmoore team was playing, but more important than the game was the quality time I was having with my son. I held the rank of Agent-In-Charge over the Oklahoma City enforcement division. A year later, I would be the agency Director and the head of the organization. It was a holiday, Veteran's Day, and I was off work. We had a laidback day, and planned to end it with some football.

Due to the cold night, I had a heavy jacket on and that hampered me feeling my bureau phone go off. I finally heard the ringtone, and I answered, "Hello?" I immediately recognized the voice on the other end as the bureau dispatch. "Darrell, there has been a shooting in Woodward. Agent Chip Engle shot a guy. Chip is all right, but the bad guy is not going to make it. Get to Woodward as soon as you can."

That was the type of call that got your blood pumping fast! We had a shooting team that consisted of four supervisors from around the state and rotated members every three months. I was on the shooting team, and it looked like I would be going to Woodward. I left the game and delivered my son safely home.

Oklahoma is a large state, and the distance between Oklahoma City and Woodward is approximately 140 miles. Moore is a suburb of Oklahoma City, and it is located in central Oklahoma. Woodward is located in far northwest Oklahoma. We had to arrive in Woodward as soon as possible. People and agents have a tendency to drive faster than normal, and we didn't need to have an automobile accident. Therefore, I contacted our air unit and arranged to be flown. At the time, we had an older model Queen Air, which was well maintained and was much faster than driving. Our pilot was a retired full bird Colonel in the military, and I had the utmost confidence we would arrive safely. The team consisted of two other agents, the pilots, and me.

We lifted off into the night sky with a million thoughts running through my mind. I was glad Chip was all right. I was gathering my thoughts as what we would find, the circumstances surrounding today's events, and the shooting. The crazy world of narcotics enforcement had struck again. One moment I was at a football game and enjoying time with my son, the next moment on a plane going to a crime scene. I quietly asked my Lord to help me as we cut through the evening sky. My God is faithful, and I had great confidence that He was with me in the air, and He would be by my side as we landed. For no matter what, my Father was on the throne.

We landed safely at the Woodward airport. We had several local agents meet us to assist us with ground transportation. As we exited the aircraft, I noticed the night was dark, and the air had gotten colder. Woodward is notoriously colder than Oklahoma City due to its location. Only the few lights surrounding the small, but adequate, airport pierced the murkiness.

As we walked across the tarmac, we received shocking news. Agent Engle was injured much more severely than expected and was being airlifted via medical helicopter to an Oklahoma City hospital. I was unclear what his injuries were, but we were told it didn't look like he was going to make it. We were stunned. The only word prior to this was that he was fine, and now the situation had taken a 180 degree turn. An agent's life was now in peril. They also briefed that the bad guy, Lynn Vaughn, had been shot one time and was in serious condition. It appeared that Vaughn would survive, but would likely be paralyzed.

The news took its toll on the shooting team immediately, and all I could think about was the family of Agent Engle. He had a wonderful wife and three children at home. "Oh please Lord, let Chip live!" I plead. I thought about what a strong Christian faith Chip had, and how none of this made sense as the drivers took us to the scene. I am glad it took several minutes from the airport to the actual scene after hearing the troubling news. I needed those valuable minutes to regroup and refocus on the task at hand.

I had to realize the best thing I could do for Chip at this point was to do my job at the highest level and find out the facts of the incident. Chip was a solid man, devoted father, and an exceptional law enforcement officer. He had been in this profession for several years, starting in small-town Oklahoma, and had been an Oklahoma Bureau of Narcotics agent for five years.

As we approached the scene, I could see several law enforcement vehicles with their emergency lights still engaged. I stepped out of the vehicle and was greeted immediately by a longtime friend and member of the Oklahoma Highway Patrol. He was a personal friend of Agent Engle, and I could see the hurt in his eyes as he described what he saw that evening. He was one of the first to get the call and respond. He found Chip in the ditch, unresponsive. It didn't look good.

It was just before midnight now and several hours had passed since the original incident. We walked through the crime scene and started piecing it together. Agent Engle's vehicle was in the middle of the dirt road and his emergency lights were still activated. The door of his truck was open. We then walked across the road a short distance to a spot in the ditch where Agent Engle was recovered. I could see his boots, his Glock pistol, and his spurs. Yes, spurs. You see, Chip always said he was a cowboy first and a cop second. He didn't wear a cowboy hat as an undercover prop; he was a true cowboy. He had spent his day off with his children riding horses.

Some images in life you never forget and stay with you as long as you live. This was one of those times in my life. You hear about law enforcement tragedies all the time, but the reality is they are not just a badge number or a uniform. They are human beings with lives, hopes, dreams, families, hobbies, and a future. They laugh and cry. They have children they adore. Seeing Chip's boots, gun, hat, and spurs was almost unbearable and forever etched in my memory.

We continued from the ditch and walked toward a pickup that had traveled through the front yard of a residence and crashed into a tree. The truck had perfectly driven between two posts, which frankly looked almost impossible considering how tight the clearance appeared. As we approached the crashed vehicle, I noticed it was not running, but its lights had been left on. The lights were eerily dimming. It was a chilling backdrop.

The interior of the vehicle was trashy with papers comingled with cans and other debris. We saw no apparent clues to what happened earlier in the evening. The pickup could not tell us the story.

The command post was set up for warmth for all the law enforcement on the scene. Oklahoma's fall weather can be chilling and the northwest area is more windy and colder than other parts of the state. The tedious task was in motion to decide what had happened on this blustery Friday night. Although, Chip and his status were in the forefront of everyone's thoughts.

When a crisis happens, the enemy starts putting questions in our minds with the objective of creating spiritual doubt. Why does something like this happen to such good people? Agent Engle is a Christ follower and shouldn't God have protected him?

If anyone in your life ever acts like they have all the answers to these questions, then they are wiser than I am. All I do know is that we will not have a clear picture until we see the Lord in heaven and can ask why. Be careful of anyone who thinks he completely knows the mind of our God.

My faith is that we will see His plan clearly one day, and God's plan will come together. I do know God is sovereign. God is El Shaddai, the Almighty God. He is omnipotent, thus His power is unlimited, and He is able to do anything.

Isaiah 55:8-9 (NIV) says, *"For my thoughts are not your thoughts, neither are your ways my ways, declares the Lord. As the heavens are higher than the earth, so are my ways higher than your ways and my thoughts than your thoughts."* Don't let anyone fool you, we can't totally understand God.

The details started to come to light about how the tragedy unfolded. You have to remember that Woodward's population is approximately 13,000 people. Everyone knows everyone, and it is difficult to keep the identities of the agents and their families secret. Wives and children of narcotics agents who work in small communities are always on the alert for suspicious people who may be following them or staking out an office or personal residence.

Chip had worked horses all day with his family. He loved horses and was a cowboy through and through. After a long day of riding and enjoying his wife and three young kids, Agent Engle's wife left in the evening to get dinner. On her way back home, an individual started following her. Their residence was in the country, and it took specific effort to find it. It was on a sparsely populated stretch of rural Oklahoma.

Yet the individual made turn after turn as he followed Agent Engle's wife and children. She had been an officer's wife for many years, and she knew something wasn't right. She didn't recognize the vehicle nor the driver, and the butterflies in her stomach now had turned to fear. She sensed danger. She thought if she could only get home to her husband, everything would be okay. Agent Engle was a tough man, and he would do anything to protect his family.

Finally, she made it home. As she sped into the driveway, the pickup was still behind her, and it slowly pulled into the driveway. She rushed into the house and told Chip that a stranger was following her and had driven into their driveway.

Chip immediately grabbed his bureau-issued firearm and raced out the door to confront the stalker. He jumped into his bureau-issued pickup and sped out of the driveway. The suspect had pulled out of the driveway and was making his way down the dirt road. Chip pulled in behind him and activated his red emergency light. The vehicle stopped in the road. Chip's vehicle was strategically and properly located behind him for the traffic stop.

Chip then approached the vehicle and by all indications confronted the driver. The driver then for some unknown reason accelerated the pickup while Agent Engle was standing in the door. Agent Engle was then being dragged by the vehicle. In a split second, the agent was in a life or death situation. Agent Engle then shot one round from his agency-issued Glock. It struck the driver and immediately lodged in his spinal column. The driver was immediately paralyzed.

Agent Engle was hanging on the vehicle for dear life and was slung to the ground as the vehicle spun out of control through the ditch. The jolt of the trench was too much for Agent Engle to hang on and he fell violently to the ground, hitting his head.

The vehicle with the injured assailant slowly decelerated and came to rest against the tree. The confrontation was over. Agent Engle was taken to a local hospital in an unconscious state. The medical officials then determined that Agent Engle's brain was swelling and needed advanced care in order to survive. He was then airlifted to Mercy Hospital in Oklahoma City in an attempt to save his life.

The bureau was in total grief for Chip and his family. The prayers were flowing as our team finished the preliminary investigation, and I drove back to Oklahoma City. The Engle family had flown on the bureau aircraft to Oklahoma City to be with Chip. I was tired, and driving was a challenge, but all I could think of was the survival of Chip and what his family was going through that night.

I arrived at Mercy hospital and found the ICU unit. I am always so proud of law enforcement and how they take care of each other and stick by one another's side. The bureau had agents assigned around the clock in support of the family. We brought our mobile command post to the hospital as a place for people to get away and rest as they supported the family.

I went in to see Chip, and it saddened me. He was unconscious and had a variety of tubes, wires, and monitors hooked to him. This was a good, Christian man who loved his wife and his three small children. I had to stay in continued prayer for the family. It's easy to blame or question God, but you can't allow yourself to do it.

The days were long as we clung to hope. Proverbs 13:12 (NIV) says, *"Hope deferred makes the heart sick."* We would tie another knot on the end of the rope and hold on to the doctors' words while we waited for Chip to show signs that he was coming out of the coma.

Midway during the week, the doctors began to communicate to the family that the end may be coming soon. One evening as many of the bureau agents lined the hallways and filled the waiting room, we braced for Chip's three small children to come say "goodbye" to their father, their hero.

They were young children, and it broke my heart to see them. The son in his cowboy hat was a spitting image of his dad. The two little girls were dressed up to see their father. They were saying goodbye. My children were similar in ages, and it was almost more than I could stand. I had to walk away for a moment and get my composure.

I think sometimes we think that Christians are not to hurt or ever to cry, but remember our Lord stood at the tomb of Lazarus and wept. He knew

He could raise him from the dead, but yet He showed emotion at the sight of Lazarus' family in such a state of pain.

On November 18, exactly one week after the incident, at approximately 5:00 pm, Chip lost his fight, and he left this world. A good man was gone. Law enforcement from several agencies came in large numbers to pay their respects at his funeral. We were there to support the family and surround them with a bond. Law enforcement people stick together and this was no different. Chip would be missed, but never forgotten—a true American domestic hero.

We still had unfinished business. Would justice be brought to the individual who did this violent act? Lynn Vaughn was charged, but never spent significant time in jail. Witnesses said Vaughn had been using methamphetamine, and blood tests confirmed this use on the night of the incident. He was on probation from a prior drug offence. Doctors suspected that there was significant blood loss after being shot, which led to brain damage and memory loss. Thus, Vaughn was not legally competent to defend himself. He was confined to a wheelchair and was paralyzed from the gunshot wound.

After spending a significant amount of time in recovery, he was released by the State Department of Mental Health into the care of his mother. He died on September 25, 2014, in Shattuck, Oklahoma. The devil laughed again.

11

THE FINAL WORD

The drug world is an unforgiving world of hurt and pain. The world is full of addicts who wished they could take back the very moment they took their first taste of the devil's candy. Lives are destroyed every day. I have witnessed it first hand, and it's not pretty, but that is NOT the final word. We have someone fighting for us, and He is greater than the enemy. I am living proof of His power and strength. But more importantly, this is what the Bible says about our Jesus, who is on the right hand of the Father making intercession for us: Advocate, Lamb of God, the Resurrection and Life, Shepherd and Bishop of Souls, Judge, Lord of Lords, Man of Sorrows, Head of Church, Master, Faithful and True Witness, Rock, High Priest, the Door, Living Water, Bread of Life, Rose of Sharon, Alpha and Omega, True Vine, Messiah, Teacher, Holy One, Mediator, the Beloved, Branch, Carpenter, Good Shepherd, Light of the World, Image of the Invisible God, The Word, Chief Cornerstone, Savior, Servant, Author and Finisher of our Faith, the Almighty, Everlasting Father, Shiloh, Lion of the Tribe of Judah, I Am, King of Kings, Prince of Peace, Bridegroom, Only Begotten Son, Wonderful

Counselor, Immanuel, Son of Man, Dayspring, the Amen, King of the Jews, Prophet, Redeemer, Anchor, Bright Morning Star, the Way, the Truth and the Life. Our Jesus.

The greatest decision I have ever made in my life was when I gave my heart to Christ. The plan is simple. The Bible says in Romans 10:9 (NIV), *"7If you declare with your mouth, 'Jesus is Lord,' and believe in your heart that God raised him from the dead, you will be saved."* Salvation is not about complex religion but the simplicity of a relationship with our Lord. The eternal consequences of this decision are out of this world.

Made in the USA
San Bernardino, CA
21 March 2017